AWESOME ACTIVITIES FOR SUPER HEROES

By Sarah Parvis

downtown bookworks

Downtown Bookworks Inc.
265 Canal Street
New York, NY 10013
www.downtownbookworks.com

Special thanks: Maccabee Katz, Michelle Pereira

Katana illustrations on pages 38, 57, 70, 129, and 147 and
Bumblebee illustrations on pages 80, 130, 136, 156, and 158 by Scott Kolins.

Mazes and jigsaw puzzle shapes courtesy of Savgraf/Shutterstock.com (pages 4–5, 38), brovkin/Shutterstock.com (page 18), Volonoff/Shutterstock.com (pages 19, 41), PhotoNAN/Shutterstock.com (page 34), Petr Bukal/Shutterstock.com (pages 53, 125), katarina_1/Shutterstock.com (page 64), Igor Zakowski/Shutterstock.com (page 102), DVARG/Shutterstock.com (pages 111, 124), VOOK/Shutterstock.com (pages 130–131), Khaladok/Shutterstock.com (page 136), Nadja Gellermann/Shutterstock.com (page 144).

Designed by Georgia Rucker

Printed in China, June 2017

ISBN: 978-1-941367-40-7

10 9 8 7 6 5 4 3 2 1

HEY ROBIN, WANT TO BOOST YOUR BRAINPOWER?
ALWAYS!
READY, SET, GO!

Dragon Race!
OH NO! A TERRIFYING MONSTER IS ON THE LOOSE DOWNTOWN.
Superman can outfly a supersonic jet. Supergirl also has Kryptonian super-speed. And The Flash is the Fastest Man Alive. Which one of these brave super heroes will battle the ferocious dragon? Follow the paths to find out.

WHAT HAPPENS WHEN THE SUPER HERO REACHES THE DRAGON?
BOR-ING!

Fly by Night

Batman uses his Batrope to zoom quickly from place to place. What is his Batrope attached to? What is Batman swinging toward? Use your doodling powers!

BOO!
Yes!
Catwoman will you Marry me!!
Jupiter
Stop
No!
POO

Robot Remodeling

The Man of Steel took on a pair of pesky robots, and they are going to need spare parts, for sure. Find seven things that have been rearranged.

Say What?

Billy Batson wasn't born with superpowers. But when he utters a magic word, he transforms into an unstoppable force for good, with the wisdom of Solomon, the strength of Hercules, the stamina of Athens, the power of Zeus, the courage of Achilles, and the speed of Mercury. And the magic word is **SHAZAM!**

IF SHOUTING ONE WORD COULD GIVE YOU UNBEATABLE SUPERPOWERS, WHAT WOULD THE WORD BE?

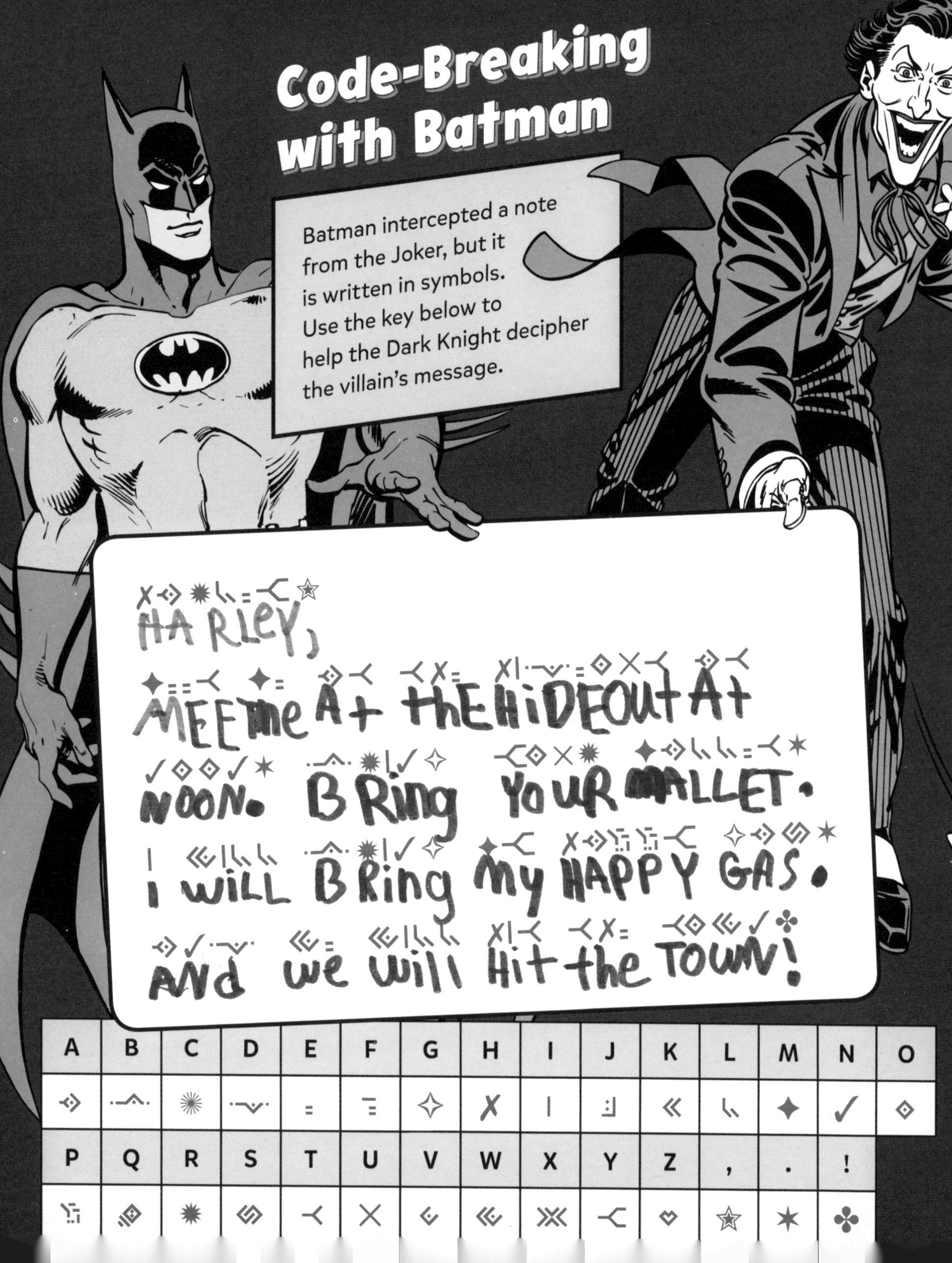

Code-Breaking with Batman
Batman intercepted a note from the Joker, but it is written in symbols. Use the key below to help the Dark Knight decipher the villain's message.
A B C D E F G H I J K L M N O
P Q R S T U V W X Y Z , . !

WONDER
WOMAN

HO! HA!
HO!
HO!
HO!
HA!
HA!
HA!
HA!
HA!
HO!
HO!
HO!
HA!
HA!
THE Joker

Once a Trickster, Always a Trickster

Harley Quinn can't stay still. Even her pictures are on the move! See what's shifted from one picture to the next. There are eight changes.

Test Your Memory

Study this picture for 30 seconds. Then turn the page and see how many questions you can answer correctly.

Is Your Memory Shipshape or Shoddy?

Look at the picture on page 15 for 30 seconds and then answer these questions. Are your eyes as keen as Superman's?

1. WHAT COLOR IS THE VEHICLE SUPERMAN IS HOLDING UP?

a. Yellow

b. Blue

c. Pink

d. Polka-dotted

2. HOW MANY PEOPLE ARE IN THE CAR?

a. 2

b. 3

c. 4

d. 5

3. IS THERE A PET IN THE CAR?

a. No.

b. Yes, a dog.

c. Yes, a cat.

d. No, but there are birds flying in the sky.

4. WHAT IS IN THE BACKGROUND?

a. A lawn with flowers

b. Trees and a lake

c. Tall mountains

d. A baseball diamond

5. WHICH OF THESE THINGS IS NOT IN THE CAR?

a. A picnic basket

b. A baseball bat

c. A woman with a hat

d. A surfboard

6. WHAT IS THE MAN IN THE DRIVER'S SEAT DOING?

a. Waving his hand

b. Playing the harmonica

c. Texting

d. Waving his hat

Imagination Station

Batgirl loves to invent new gadgets. What is she dreaming up now? How can it help her battle the bad guys?

Operation Rescue Lois

General Zod has trapped Lois Lane in the center of an intergalactic maze. Can Superman find her in time? Find a flight path that takes the Man of Steel right to her.

Justice League Jigsaw

A few pieces of this power-packed puzzle have fallen out of place! Can you match the pieces to the picture? Write the letter for each piece in the empty space.

Vrooooooooooom!
Batgirl and Robin are both daring motorcycle riders. They can speed past cars, race down alleyways, and dash after criminals quickly—and in style.
R

DESIGN YOUR VERY OWN TWO-WHEELED AWESOME-MOBILE. WHAT KINDS OF SPECIAL GADGETS DOES IT HAVE? DON'T FORGET TO ADD YOUR OWN SUPER HERO SYMBOL.

Power Ranking!

Every super hero has a different set of powers to use to battle the bad guys. Which powers would you most like to have? Rank them from **1** to **10**.

OH YEAH! This is the best power ever!

That's cool, but I wouldn't, like, trade my soul for it.

____ HEAT VISION

____ FLYING

____ SUPER-STRENGTH

____ SUPER-HEARING

____ TALKING WITH ANIMALS

____ X-RAY VISION

____ CONTROLLING THE WEATHER

____ INVISIBILITY

____ ENHANCED HEALING

____ BREATHING UNDERWATER

And what about these lesser-known powers? Rank them from **1** to **10**.

I don't really need that power, but it might be fun.

No, thanks. I'd rather not.

____ MAKING ANYONE LAUGH AT ANY TIME

____ TURNING CUPS INVISIBLE (BUT NOT THE LIQUID IN THEM)

____ SPRAYING GLITTER FROM YOUR FINGERTIPS

____ TURNING ANIMALS PURPLE

____ MAKING PEOPLE GROW REALLY WEIRD FACIAL HAIR

____ TURNING WATER INTO LEMONADE

____ TICKLING PEOPLE WITHOUT TOUCHING THEM

____ TURNING BORING SANDWICHES INTO SLIGHTLY LESS BORING SANDWICHES

____ ENHANCED STAMINA WHILE PLAYING PING-PONG

____ UNCONTROLLABLE SNEEZING WHENEVER YOU TRY TO SNEAK UP ON SOMEONE

WHAT WOULD YOUR MASK LOOK LIKE? DRAW IT HERE.

Talk Like a Super Hero

Superman unmasks a robot, Dr. Fate goes to the underworld, The Flash reads the paper faster than the speed of light, and Robin battles a time traveler . . . but what are they saying?

Scan It Like Cyborg

Do you have a super-speedy robot brain? See how quickly you can find all of the words in the word list. They can go up, down, forward, backward, and even diagonally. Set a timer. Ready, set, go!

Word List

ARMOR
COMPUTER
CYBERNETIC
EXPERIMENT
GENIUS
JUSTICE LEAGUE
MACHINE
MOTION SENSORS
RAVEN
RED EYE
ROBOT
STARFIRE
SUPERHUMAN
TECHNOLOGY
TEEN TITANS
VICTOR STONE

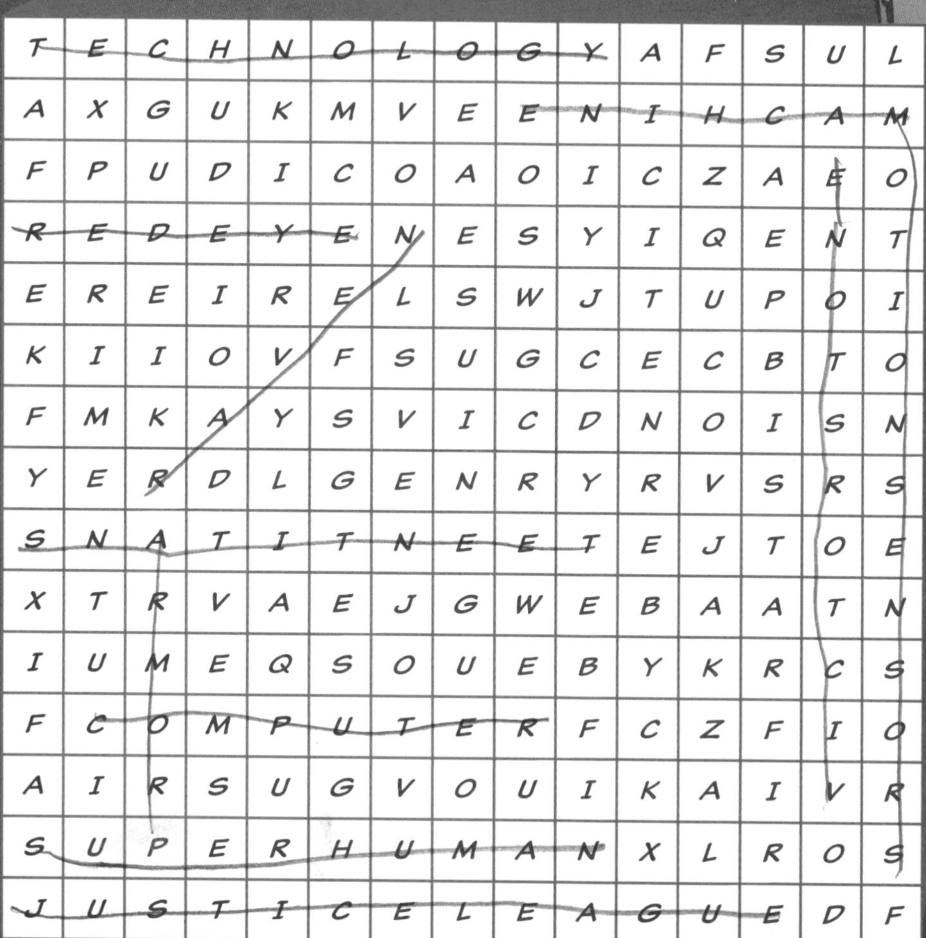

T	E	C	H	N	O	L	O	G	Y	A	F	S	U	L
A	X	G	U	K	M	V	E	E	N	I	H	C	A	M
F	P	U	D	I	C	O	A	O	I	C	Z	A	E	O
R	E	D	E	Y	E	N	E	S	Y	I	Q	E	N	T
E	R	E	I	R	E	L	S	W	J	T	U	P	O	I
K	I	I	O	V	F	S	U	G	C	E	C	B	T	O
F	M	K	A	Y	S	V	I	C	D	N	O	I	S	N
Y	E	R	D	L	G	E	N	R	Y	R	V	S	R	S
S	N	A	T	I	T	N	E	E	T	E	J	T	O	E
X	T	R	V	A	E	J	G	W	E	B	A	A	T	N
I	U	M	E	Q	S	O	U	E	B	Y	K	R	C	S
F	C	O	M	P	U	T	E	R	F	C	Z	F	I	O
A	I	R	S	U	G	V	O	U	I	K	A	I	V	R
S	U	P	E	R	H	U	M	A	N	X	L	R	O	S
J	U	S	T	I	C	E	L	E	A	G	U	E	D	F

Never Leave Home Without It

Miniature camera? Check. Fingerprint kit? Check. Tear-gas pellets, infrared flashlight, and an assortment of colored contact lenses for disguises? Check, check, and check. Batman is always prepared for anything. What would you include in your ideal Utility Belt?*

*You may need to be prepared for school, piano lessons, and soccer practice, as well as battles with villains.

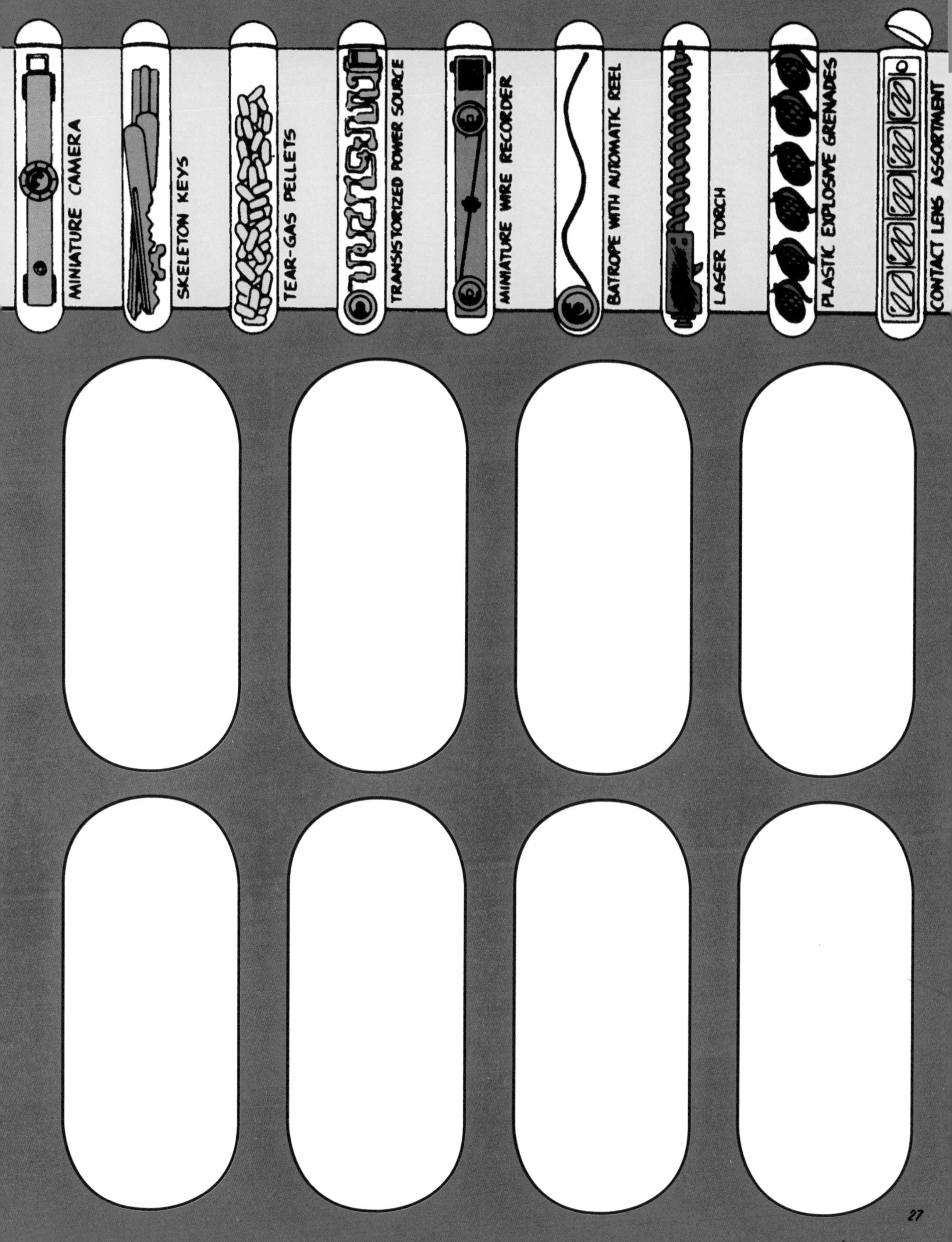
MINIATURE CAMERA
SKELETON KEYS
TEAR-GAS PELLETS
TRANSISTORIZED POWER SOURCE
MINIATURE WIRE RECORDER
BATROPE WITH AUTOMATIC REEL
LASER TORCH
PLASTIC EXPLOSIVE GRENADES
CONTACT LENS ASSORTMENT

One Too Many

Each of these puzzle pieces fits into the picture on the right, except for one. Which piece is an imposter?

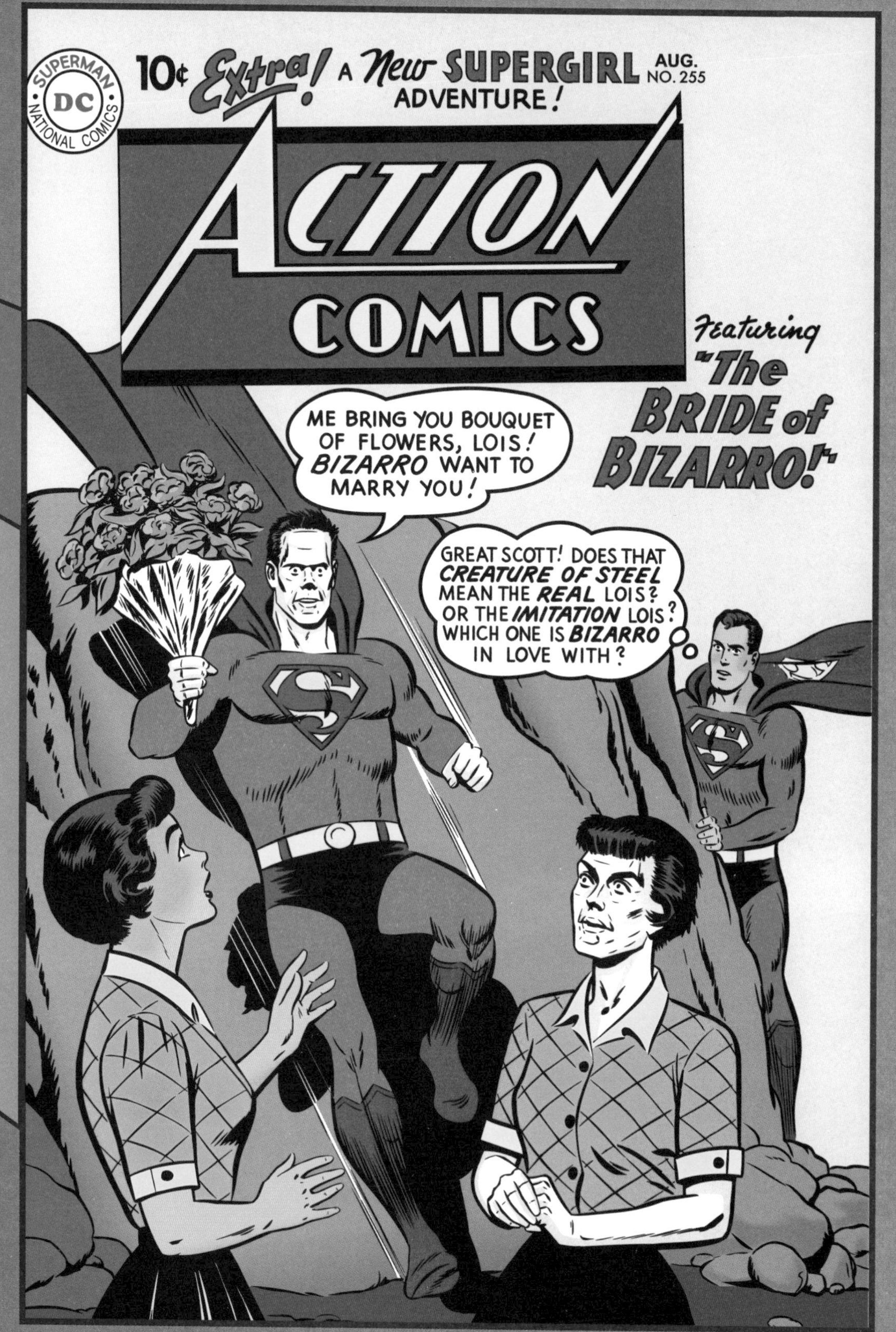
SUPERMAN DC NATIONAL COMICS
10¢ Extra! A New SUPERGIRL ADVENTURE!
AUG. NO. 255
ACTION COMICS
Featuring "The BRIDE of BIZARRO!"
ME BRING YOU BOUQUET OF FLOWERS, LOIS! BIZARRO WANT TO MARRY YOU!
GREAT SCOTT! DOES THAT CREATURE OF STEEL MEAN THE REAL LOIS? OR THE IMITATION LOIS? WHICH ONE IS BIZARRO IN LOVE WITH?

One Mighty Half Is Missing!

Challenge your powers of observation and your mastery of a pencil. Fill in the rest of the half-drawn heroes.

Use Your Eagle Eyes

Hawkman is on the move, and so are the things in this picture. Can you spot the six things that have changed?

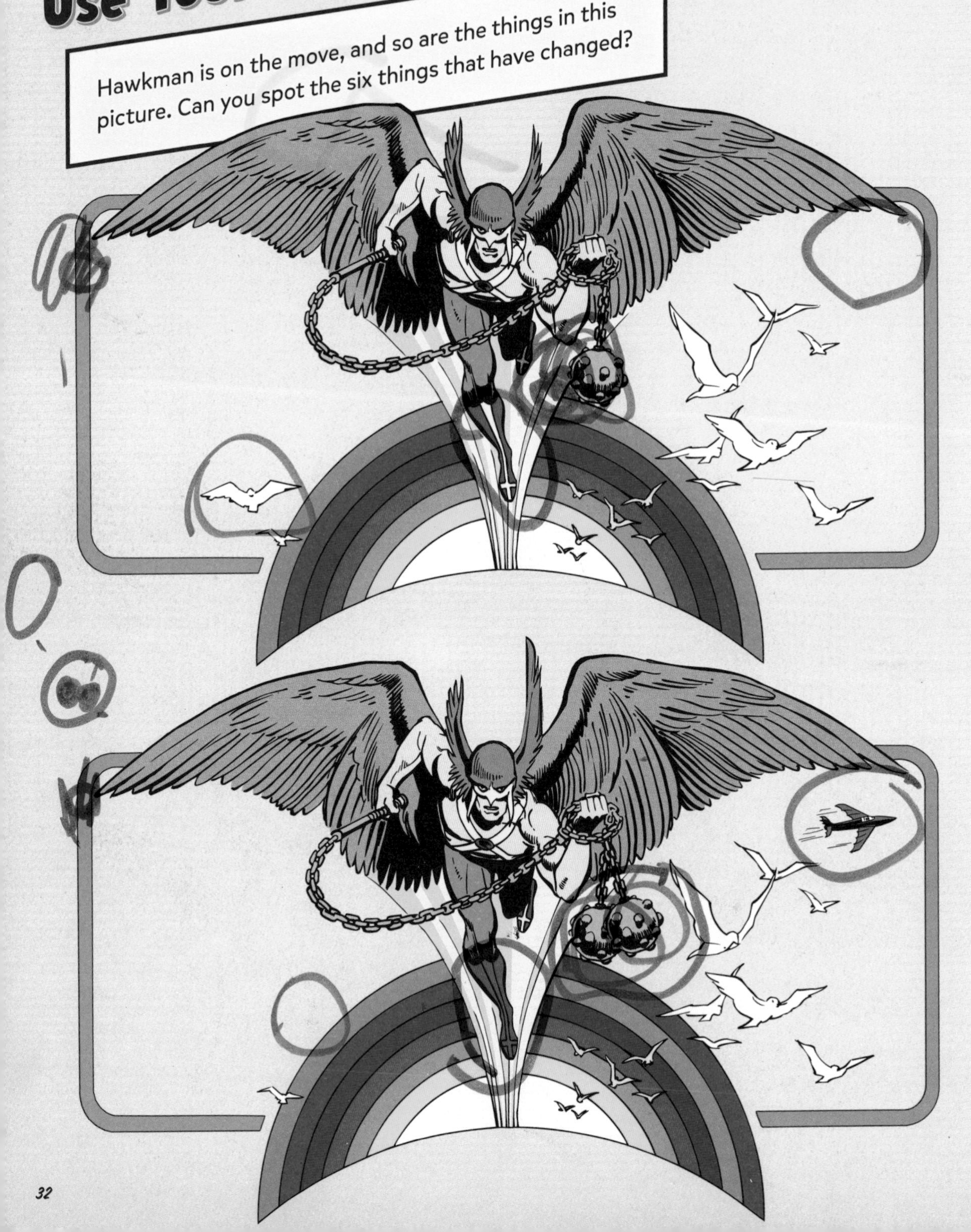

Shadow People

Sometimes super-villains lurk in the shadows. It's best to be able to spot them, no matter how well they are hidden. Can you match these shadows to the correct shady character?

Journey to the Joker

Batman has to reach the Joker before this cunning criminal puts his dastardly plan in motion.

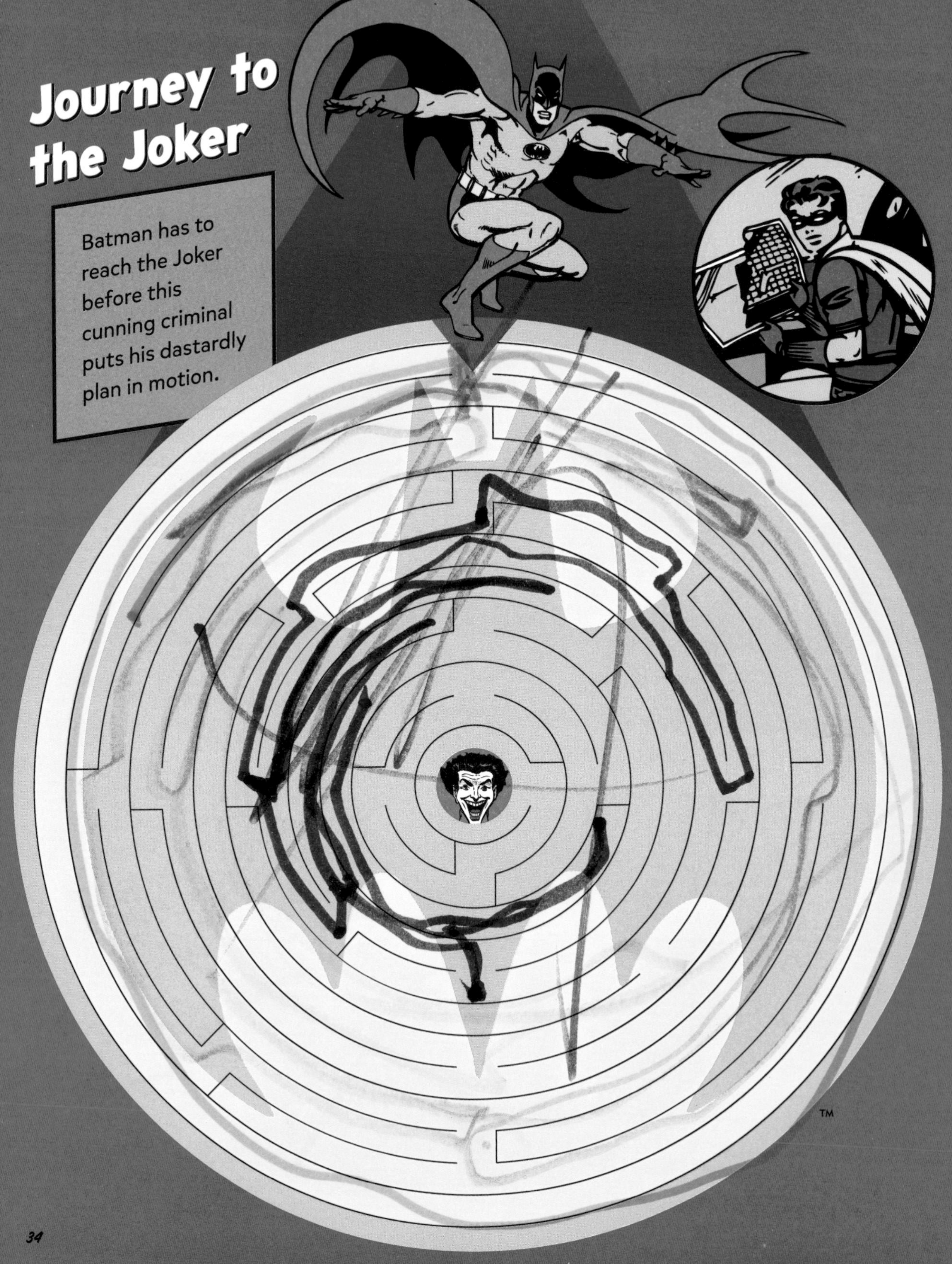

Think Like a Super Hero

What does Superman see in the factory? How can he save the day? Fill in his thoughts.

Follow the Pattern

Follow the pattern on the right to help the Justice League find some sneaky bad guys. You can go right, left, up, and down—but not diagonally. And stay away from the Joker!

THE PATTERN

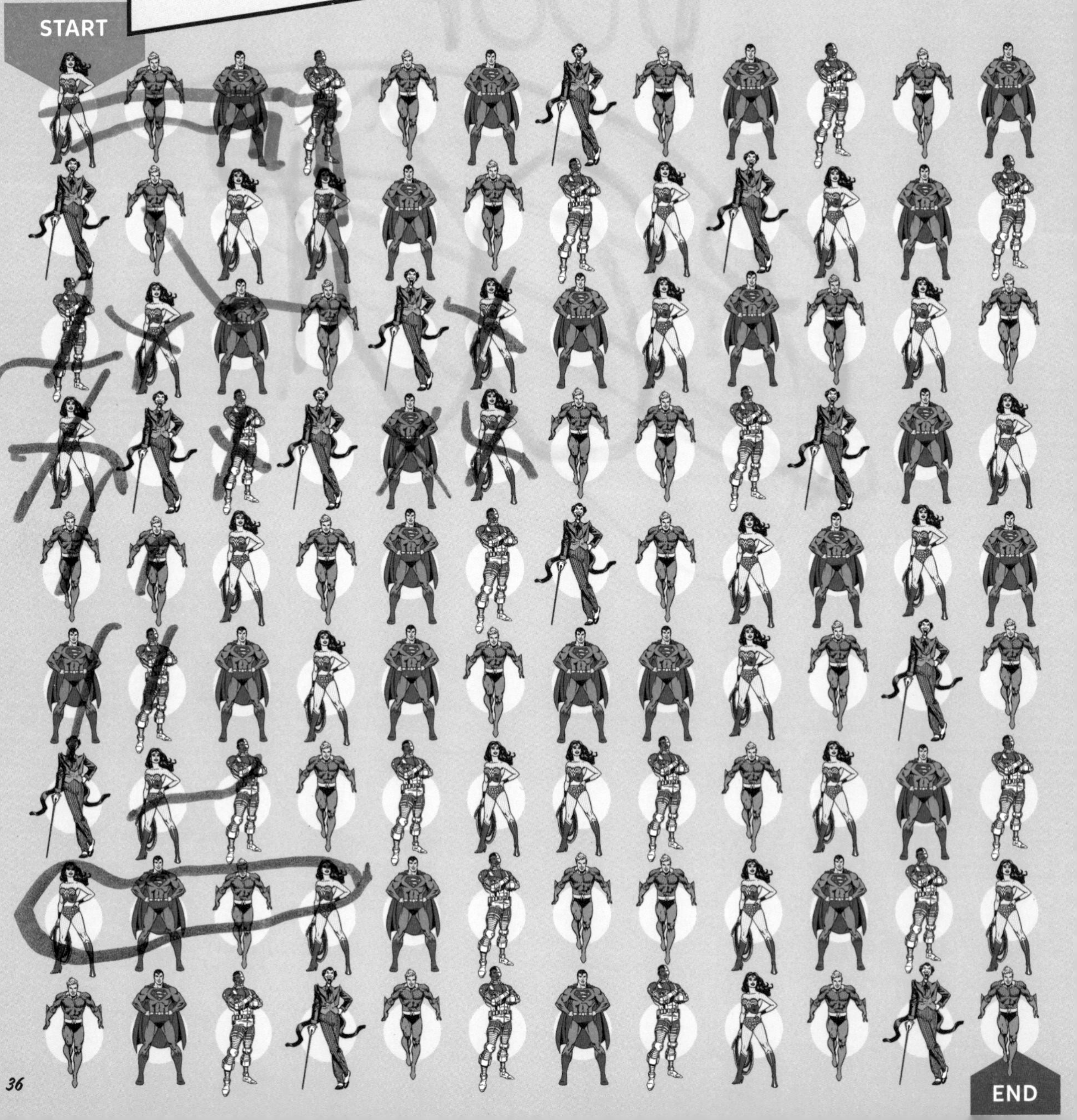

START

END

Machine Meltdown!

Wonder Woman never shies away from a fight, even when her opponent is a 10-legged robot bent on destruction. Wait, how many legs? Look closely and you will see that nine things are different in these two pictures.

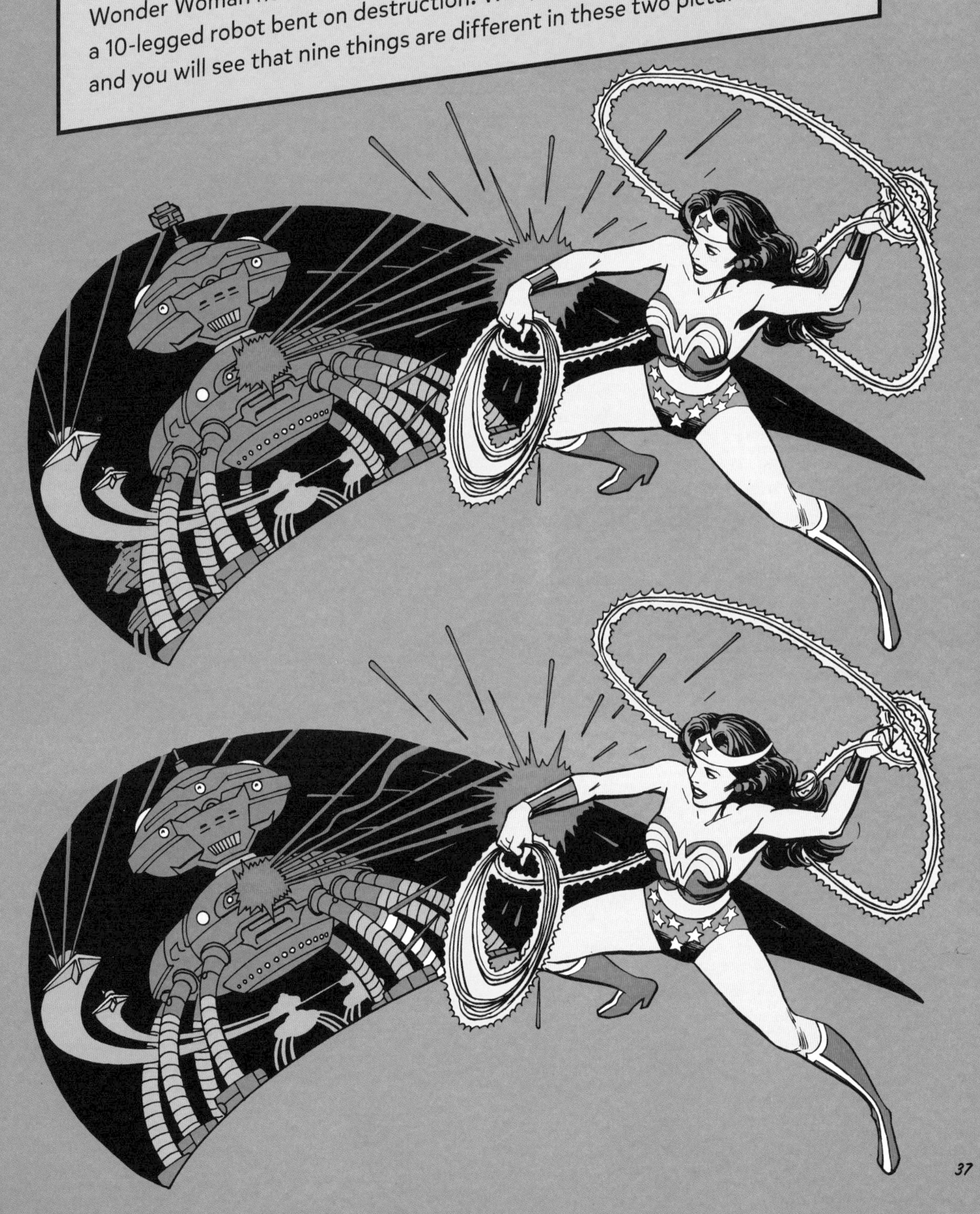

Catch That Bird!

The Penguin is terrorizing Gotham City from atop a terrifying prehistoric bird. The Flash, Katana, and Hawkman have to capture him before it's too late. Follow the paths to find out which hero finds this birdbrain.

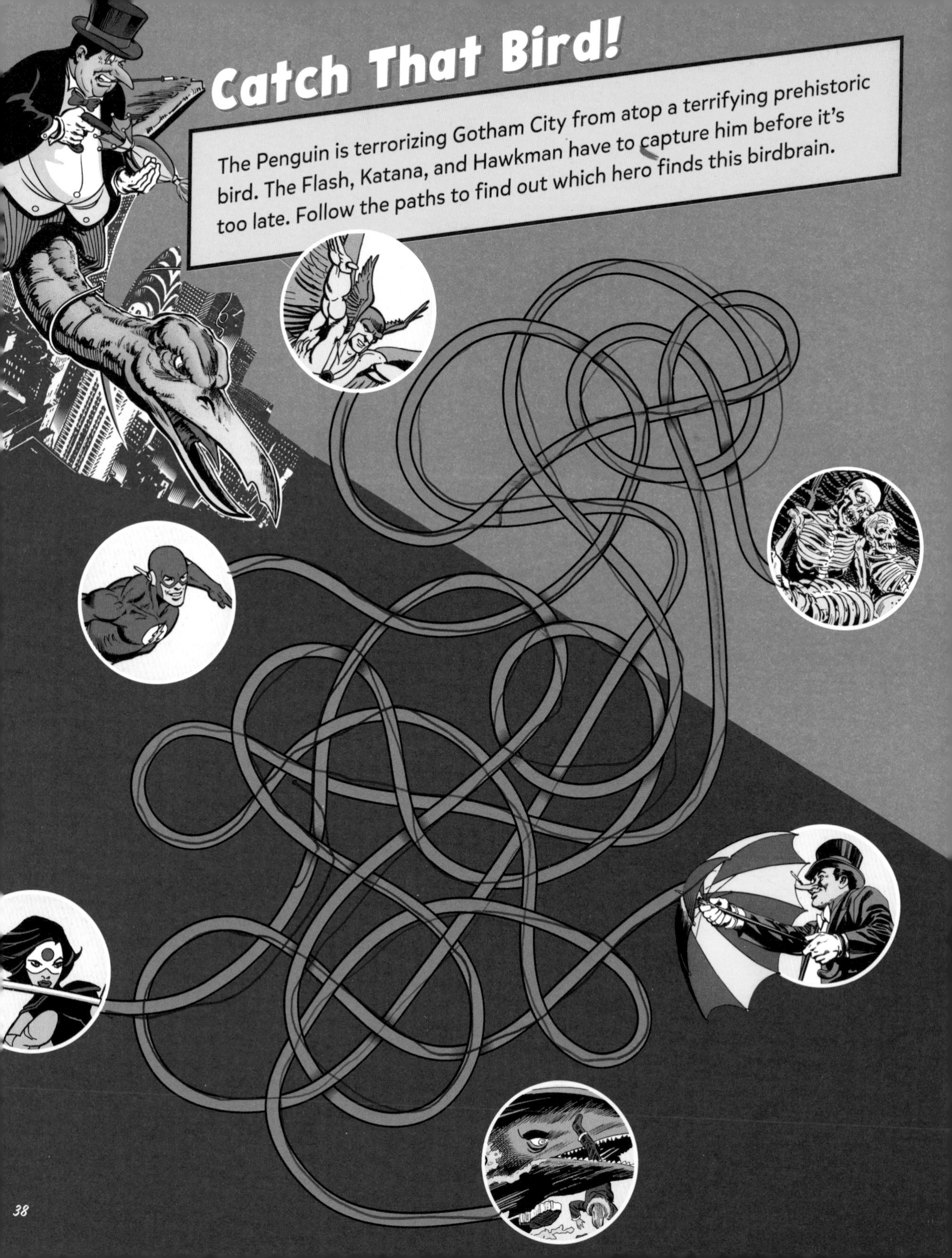

What Kind of Super Hero Would You Be?

IF YOU WERE A SUPER HERO, WOULD YOU EVER . . .

. . . TAKE A DAY OFF?

YES NO

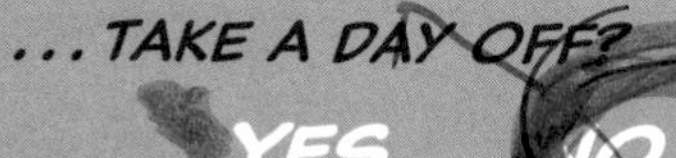

. . . USE YOUR ABILITY TO TALK TO ANIMALS TO TEACH SQUIRRELS HOW TO DANCE THE TANGO?

YES NO

. . . DEMAND TO GET PAID FOR SAVING PEOPLE?

YES NO

. . . WEAR A GIANT BACKPACK SO YOUR FRIENDS COULD CLIMB IN AND FLY AROUND THE WORLD WITH YOU?

YES NO

. . . USE YOUR SUPERPOWERS TO MAKE HUGE SANDCASTLES AT THE BEACH?

YES NO

. . . DISGUISE YOURSELF AS A REGULAR PERSON SO YOU COULD WIN TRACK AND FIELD MEDALS?

YES NO

. . . GO ON A REALITY SHOW?

YES NO

. . . LET A BAD GUY GO IF HE SAID HE WAS REALLY, REALLY SORRY?

YES NO

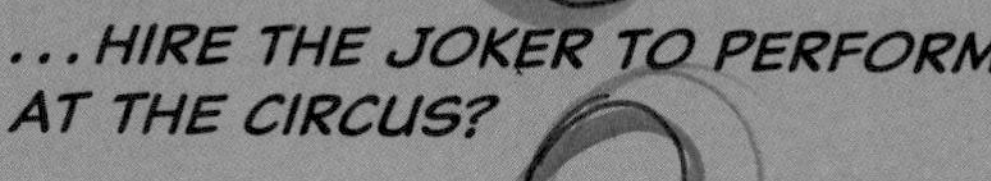

. . . HIRE THE JOKER TO PERFORM AT THE CIRCUS?

YES NO

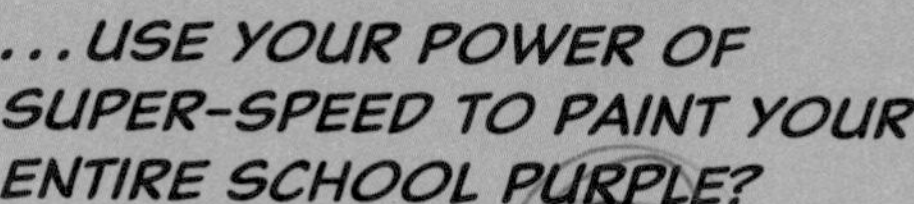

. . . USE YOUR POWER OF SUPER-SPEED TO PAINT YOUR ENTIRE SCHOOL PURPLE?

YES NO

. . . NOT SAVE SOMEONE BECAUSE HE OR SHE WAS RUDE?

YES NO

. . . USE YOUR POWERS OF TELEKINESIS TO MOVE YOUR FRIEND'S PHONE OUT OF REACH EVERY TIME HE OR SHE GOES TO PICK IT UP?

YES NO

. . . PRETEND TO BE SICK TO STAY IN YOUR SECRET HIDEOUT AND PLAY VIDEO GAMES?

YES NO

. . . USE YOUR ENHANCED SENSES TO WIN COOKING CONTESTS?

YES NO

Shape-Shifters

Sometimes battling intergalactic baddies can put some serious strain on a super hero. Even when they are bent out of shape, they shake it off afterward. Match these warped super heroes to their normal looks.

After Them!

Put the finishing touches on this Justice League jigsaw puzzle by matching the unconnected pieces to the open spots in the puzzle. Write the letter for each piece in the empty space.

Photo Finish

Do you have drawing superpowers? These half-baked heroes need you! Draw their other half.

Live Like Deadman

Deadman can take over the body of any person on Earth. When he takes over a body, he also takes over a person's skills. If you could become someone else for a day, who would it be? What would you look like?

Zatanna's Magic Jumble
Zatanna used a magic spell against the Joker. Suddenly there was a huge explosion. When the dust settled, everything was all mixed up. Unscramble the letters to find 10 magic words.
TWIHC
RAMCH
SLELP
RKICT
NATCH
RADYZWIR
CABRAADABAR
OCHUPSCOUS
CYROSER
SLINOUIL
HINT BOX
ABRACADABRA
CHANT
CHARM
HOCUS POCUS
ILLUSION
SORCERY
SPELL
TRICK
WITCH
WIZARDRY

BRAINIAC

SUPERMAN™

Crossword Caper
Read the clues on the right. Then write the answers in the crossword below.
WORD BOX
Adam
Battery
Bracelets
Cold
Cyborg
Dr. Fate
Harley
Hawkman
Joker
Krypto
Mask
Metropolis
Night
Oath
Paradise Island
Penguin
Planet
Plastic
Raven
Rocket
Tiara
Tornado
Wonder Woman
Zod

ACROSS

1. Superman is from the ________ Krypton.
3. On her head, Wonder Woman wears a ________ with a red star.
6. As a child, Superman came to Earth aboard a ________.
8. This mallet-wielding super-villain loves the Joker.
9. Being half robot gives this super hero a big brainpower boost.
13. The *Daily Planet* is the newspaper for this city where Superman lives.
16. This super-villain loves to laugh, only it is more of a crazed cackle than a sweet giggle.
17. ________ Man is a shape-shifting super hero who can hide in plain sight by assuming the form of a chair, a table, a chandelier, or anything else.
18. A Teen Titan, ________ counts magic, telekinesis, teleportation, psychic power, and the ability to manipulate shadows as some of her special skills.
19. Green Lantern recites an ________ as he recharges his power ring.
21. Black ________ is a super-villain whose quest to take over the world often pits him against Shazam!
22. ________ is a powerful sorcerer who wears a helmet, cape, and amulet.
23. Some super-villains are active during the day, but Catwoman mostly works at ________.

DOWN

1. Wonder Woman grew up on ________.
2. Captain ________ is a parka-wearing baddie with a freeze gun.
4. This bird-loving bad guy is one of Batman's worst foes.
5. His giant wings and hefty mace help this super hero solve crimes and battle super-villains.
7. Superman's loyal, crime-fighting pup is called ________.
10. Using her Golden Lasso, ________ can make even the worst criminal mastermind tell the truth.
11. A banished Kryptonian general, ________ escaped from an interdimensional prison before going after Superman.
12. Green Lantern must recharge his power ring using a special ________.
14. Shiny and indestructible, Wonder Woman's ________ can deflect bullets.
15. An android super hero, Red ________ can manipulate the wind.
20. Not every super hero wears a ________, but many do cover their faces.

Great Green Scramble

Green Lantern uses his power ring to make things out of an amazing green light. Find all of the green letters on the page and write them in the blocks below. Then unscramble them to find the missing word in his Green Lantern oath.

"IN _ _ _ _ _ _ _ _ _ DAY,
IN BLACKEST NIGHT,
NO EVIL SHALL ESCAPE MY SIGHT.
LET THOSE WHO WORSHIP EVIL'S MIGHT,
BEWARE MY POWER...
GREEN LANTERN'S LIGHT!"

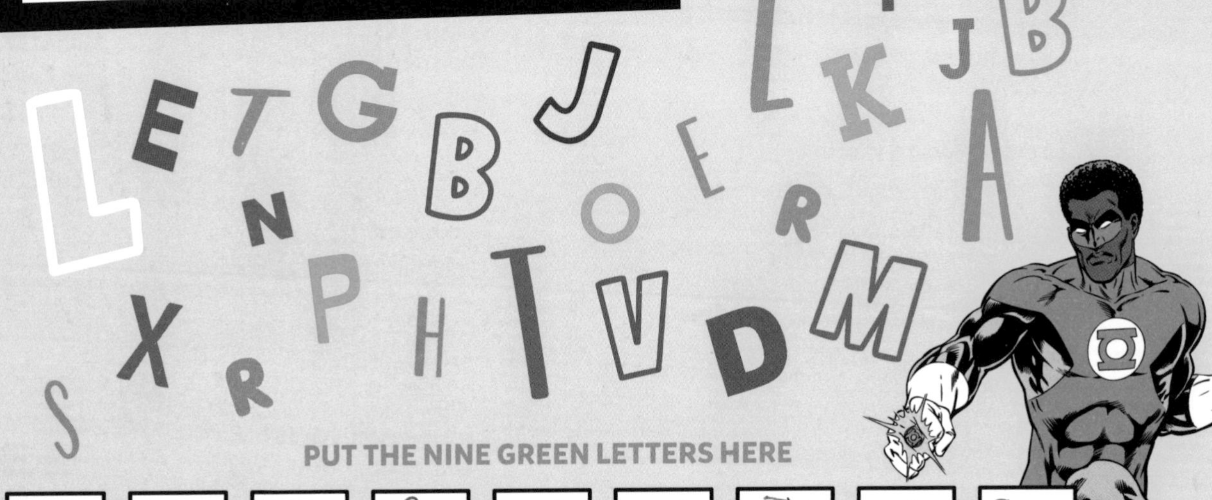

PUT THE NINE GREEN LETTERS HERE

T	E	R	B	H	T	I	S	G

Target Practice

Green Arrow practiced and practiced until he became a perfect shot. And so can you! Place the book on a table. Stand a few feet away. Toss a dime, a paper clip, or a small balled-up piece of paper (whatever small non-bouncy object you have handy) onto the target. Try it 10 times in a row and add up your score.

NOTE: YOU MIGHT WANT TO PUT A BOOK OR ANOTHER OBJECT ON TOP OF PAGE 50 TO HOLD THE BOOK OPEN.

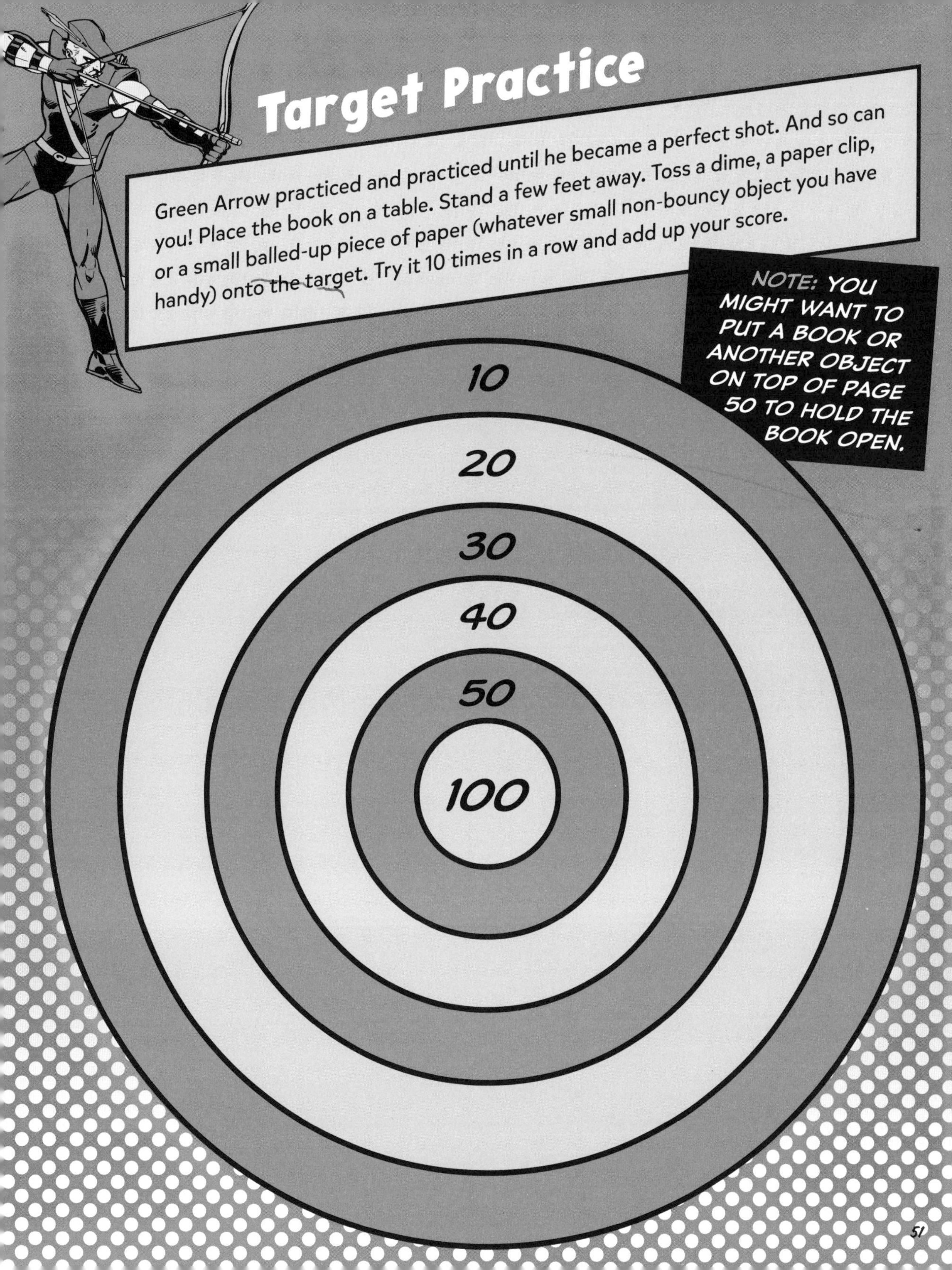

Batman and Robin

This powerful pair solves crimes and captures bad guys using their supreme intellect, martial arts skills, and amazing gadgets.

All of the words in the word list can be found in the puzzle below. They can go up, down, forward, backward, and even diagonally.

Word List

ALFRED
BATCAVE
BAT-SIGNAL
BOY WONDER
CLAYFACE
CRIME FIGHTERS
DARK KNIGHT
DYNAMIC DUO
GADGETS
MR. FREEZE
THE PENGUIN
WAYNE MANOR

Q	M	E	D	I	U	J	E	W	E	S	Y	S	O	U
U	R	S	R	E	T	H	G	I	F	E	M	I	R	C
I	F	C	L	A	Y	F	A	C	E	O	P	E	W	F
S	R	B	T	H	E	Y	D	S	T	I	X	O	A	I
K	E	A	H	P	V	U	G	P	A	E	U	G	Y	L
M	E	T	G	U	E	O	E	X	N	D	Z	T	N	D
U	Z	S	I	L	S	W	T	A	C	E	S	F	E	O
T	E	I	N	E	Q	I	S	I	M	R	C	T	M	S
D	I	G	K	S	V	Y	M	G	N	F	I	D	A	A
O	S	N	K	Q	U	A	Z	H	T	L	K	B	N	E
H	U	A	R	P	N	I	C	A	B	A	Q	A	O	S
E	N	L	A	Y	F	O	J	T	Z	V	U	I	R	Y
L	S	E	D	W	U	K	D	I	A	S	Y	W	Z	D
U	N	R	E	D	N	O	W	Y	O	B	U	P	T	E
S	B	O	I	T	H	E	P	E	N	G	U	I	N	J

Riddler's Labyrinth

Uh-oh, the Riddler is up to no good again! Batgirl, Robin, and Zatanna rush to stop him—but they have to make it through his labyrinth first. Only one path leads through the maze to the Riddler. Which super hero will confront him?

My Super Hero World

By day, Batman is Bruce Wayne, millionaire CEO of Wayne Industries, and Batgirl is Barbara Gordon, a librarian. Superman is Clark Kent, a mild-mannered reporter at the *Daily Planet*. Picture yourself as a super hero. What is your alter ego? What are your superpowers?

My alter ego name: Aariya

My alter ego job: save peple

My super hero name: wonder girl

Do I have a sidekick? **YES** (circled) **NO**

If so, here's what my sidekick is like: he is funny. good. and thoutful.

My superpowers: skating flight invincabilty can link minds make peple tell the truth with a lassor

My weakness: cookies

My arch enemy: the war god

Here is what happened once when I totally saved the day: I was flying when I saw everyone clappin but I got the war god in my ... I

NOW, DRAW YOURSELF AS A SUPER HERO.

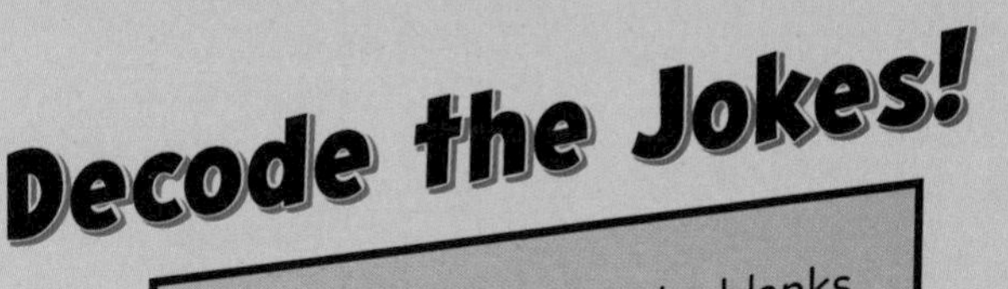

Decode the Jokes!

Use the key to fill in the blanks and uncover the answers.

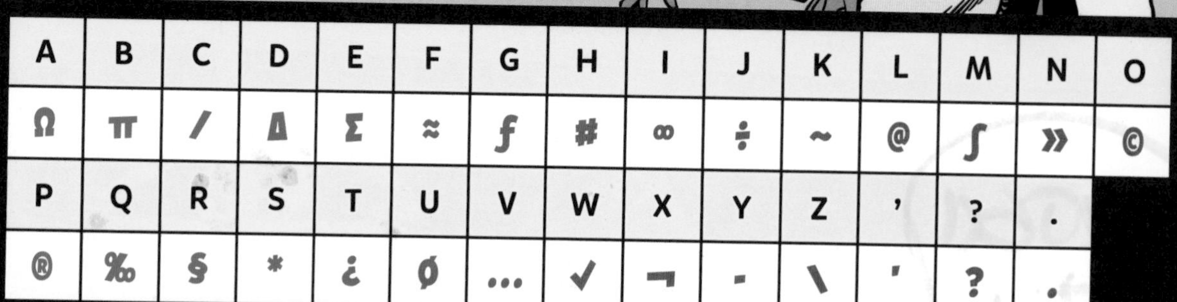

A	B	C	D	E	F	G	H	I	J	K	L	M	N	O
Ω	π	/	Δ	Σ	≈	ƒ	#	∞	÷	~	@	∫	»	©
P	Q	R	S	T	U	V	W	X	Y	Z	’	?	.	
®	‰	§	*	¿	ø	...	✓	¬	-	\	'	?	.	

What would Wonder Woman's nickname be if she were from Texas?

¿#Σ @Ω**© ≈§©∫

THE LASSO FROM

Σ@ ®Ω*©

EL PASO

What do you call Cyborg when he is on a top-secret intelligence-gathering mission?
*®-π©§ƒ
spyborg
What is Dr. Freeze's favorite dessert?
∞/Σ */§ΣΩʃ
Ice scream
What does Batman call 20 villains locked up in prison?
Ω ƒ©©∆ »∞ƒ#¿'* ✓©§~
a good night's work
How do you know Katana always does a job thoroughly and completely?
#Σ ∆©Σ»'¿ ø*Σ
#©§¿ /ø¿.
she doesn't use
shortcuts.

A Hero's Best Friend
Wonder Woman and Jumpa, Supergirl and Streaky, Superman and Krypto—super heroes have unforgettable animal friends. Who is yours? Draw your perfect pet pal. What are its superpowers?

Wonder bunny

The amaeains bunny

Super Blue

Beware of the Crocs!

Wonder Woman has her eye on the crocodiles, and so should you. But they aren't the only things changing in this pair of perilous pictures. Circle eight things that aren't the same.

Mirror Images

Make the right look just like the left to complete Firestorm and Golden Pharaoh. Then draw a scene around them.

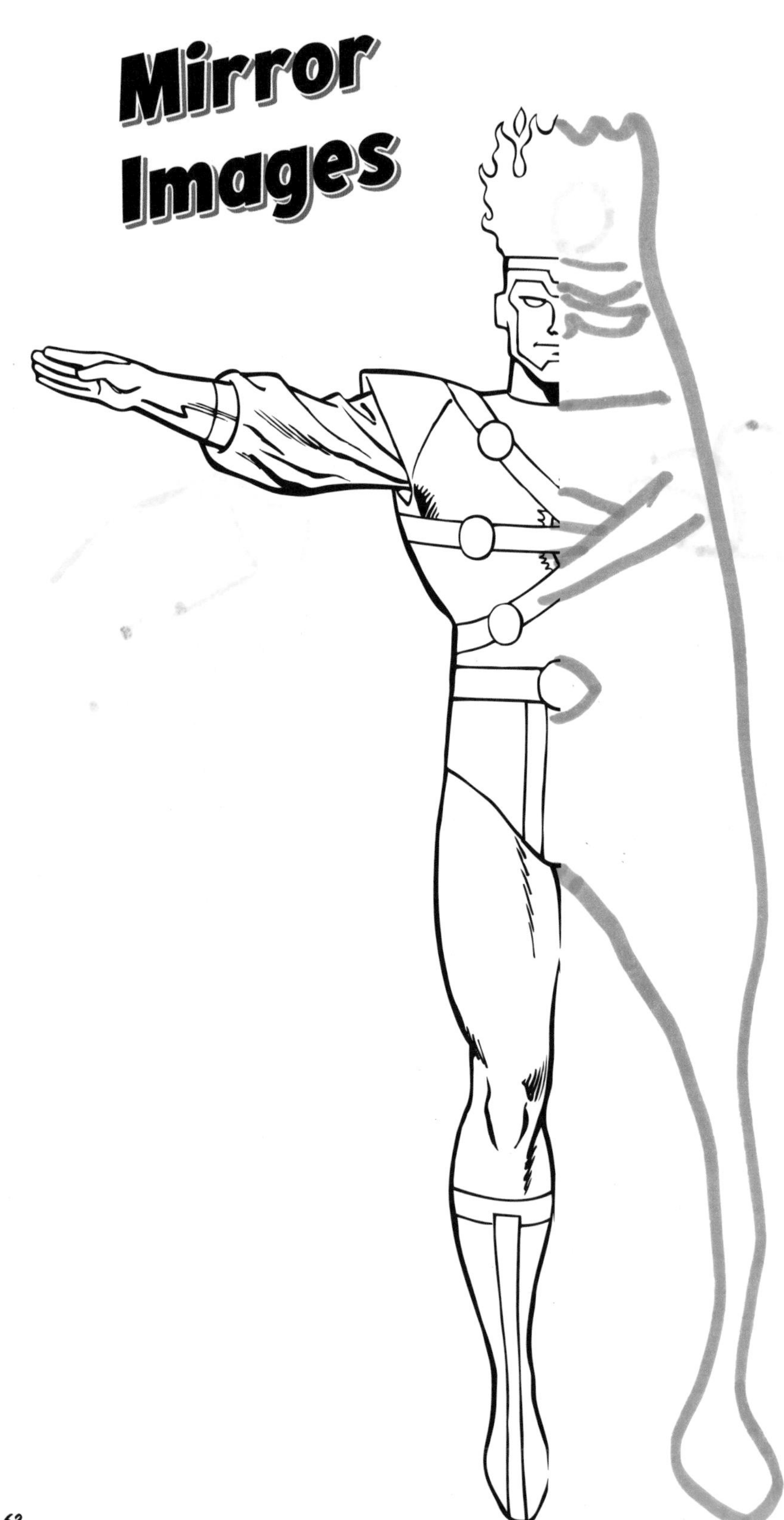

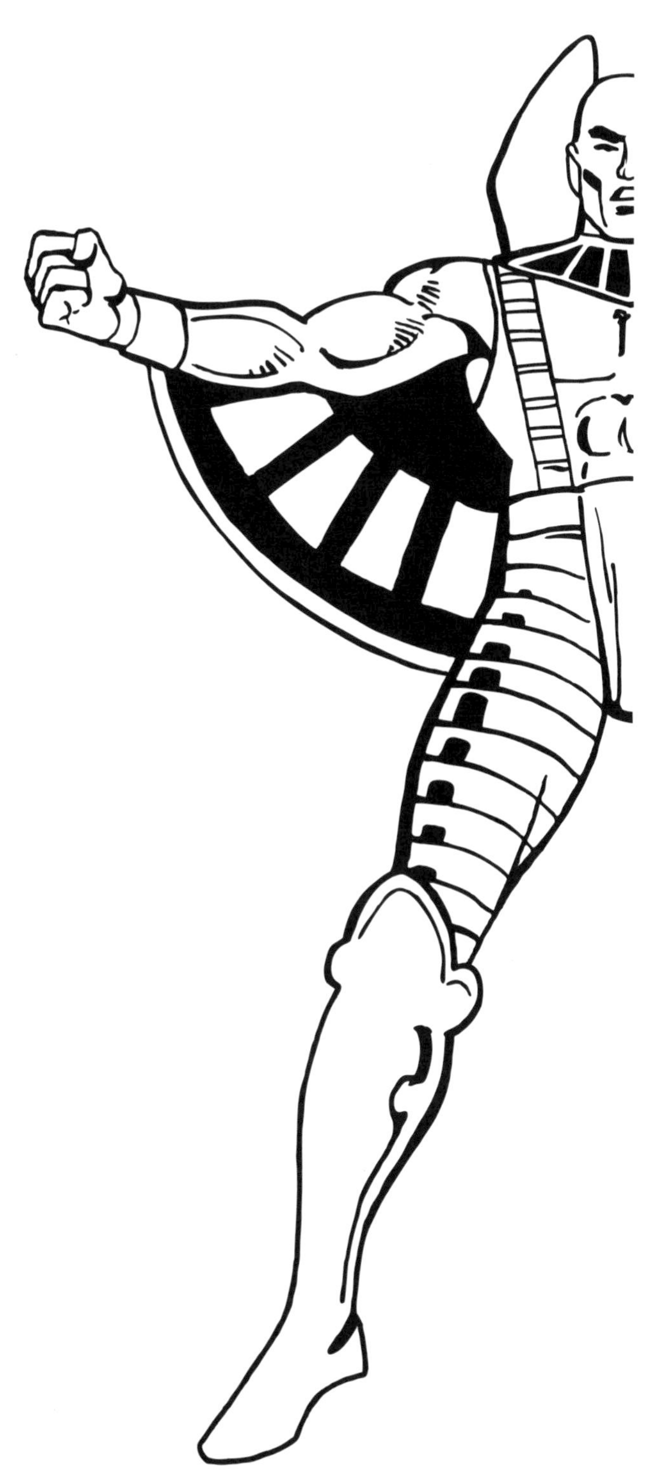

Time to Recharge!

Green Lantern needs to recharge his power ring. Guide him through the maze to reach his Power Battery.

Windblown Balderdash

Red Tornado's cyclone-force air blasts are great for battle, but they can make a mess of everything else. Help put these windblown letters back in order to make a list of words that describe super heroes.

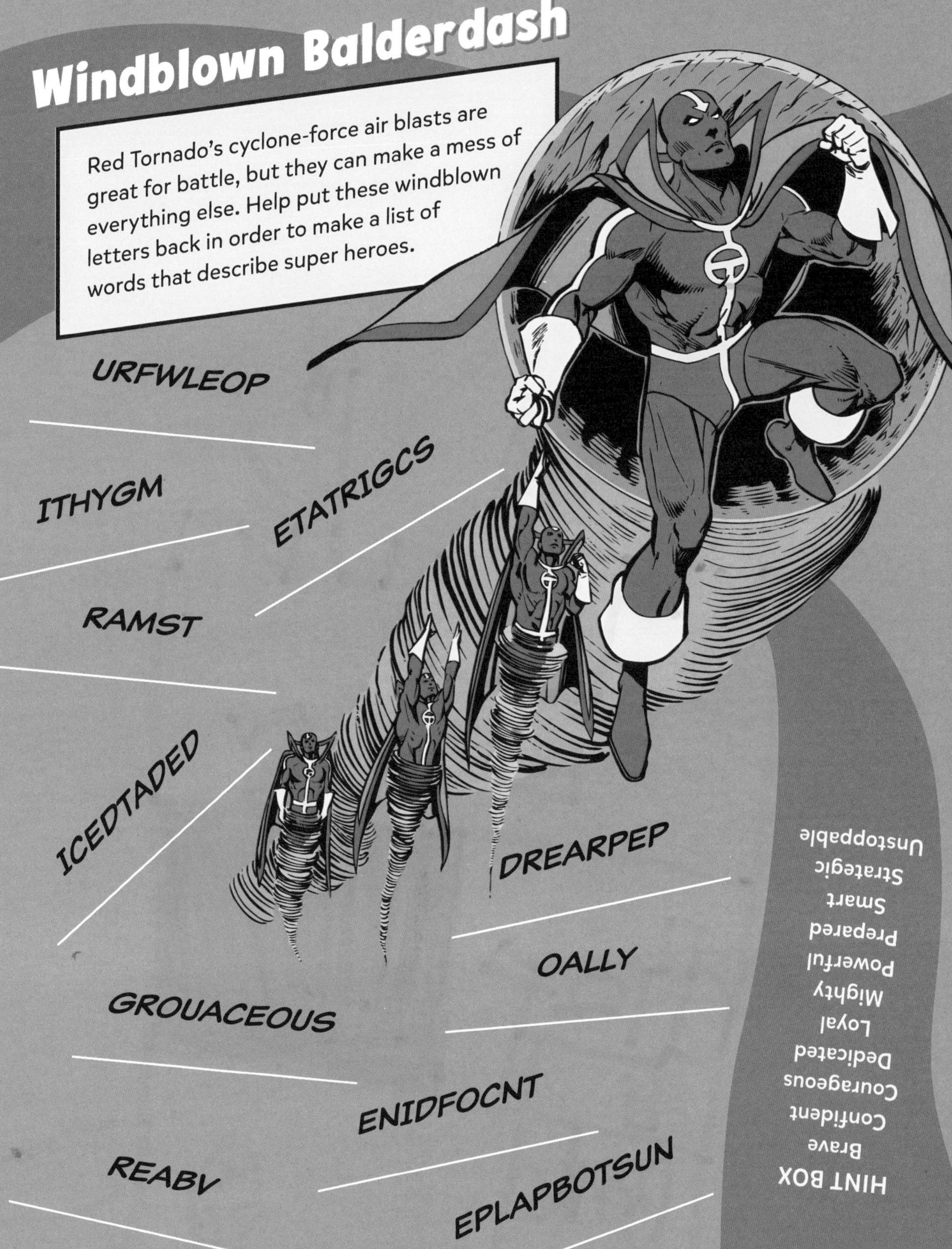

Design a Villain's Den

The Iceberg Lounge is closed for renovations, so the Penguin and his henchmen need a new secret hangout. What should his new lair look like?

P
P
P

Mismatched Pieces

Super heroes have supercharged senses. Challenge your powers of observation to find the two puzzle pieces that didn't come from the picture on the right.

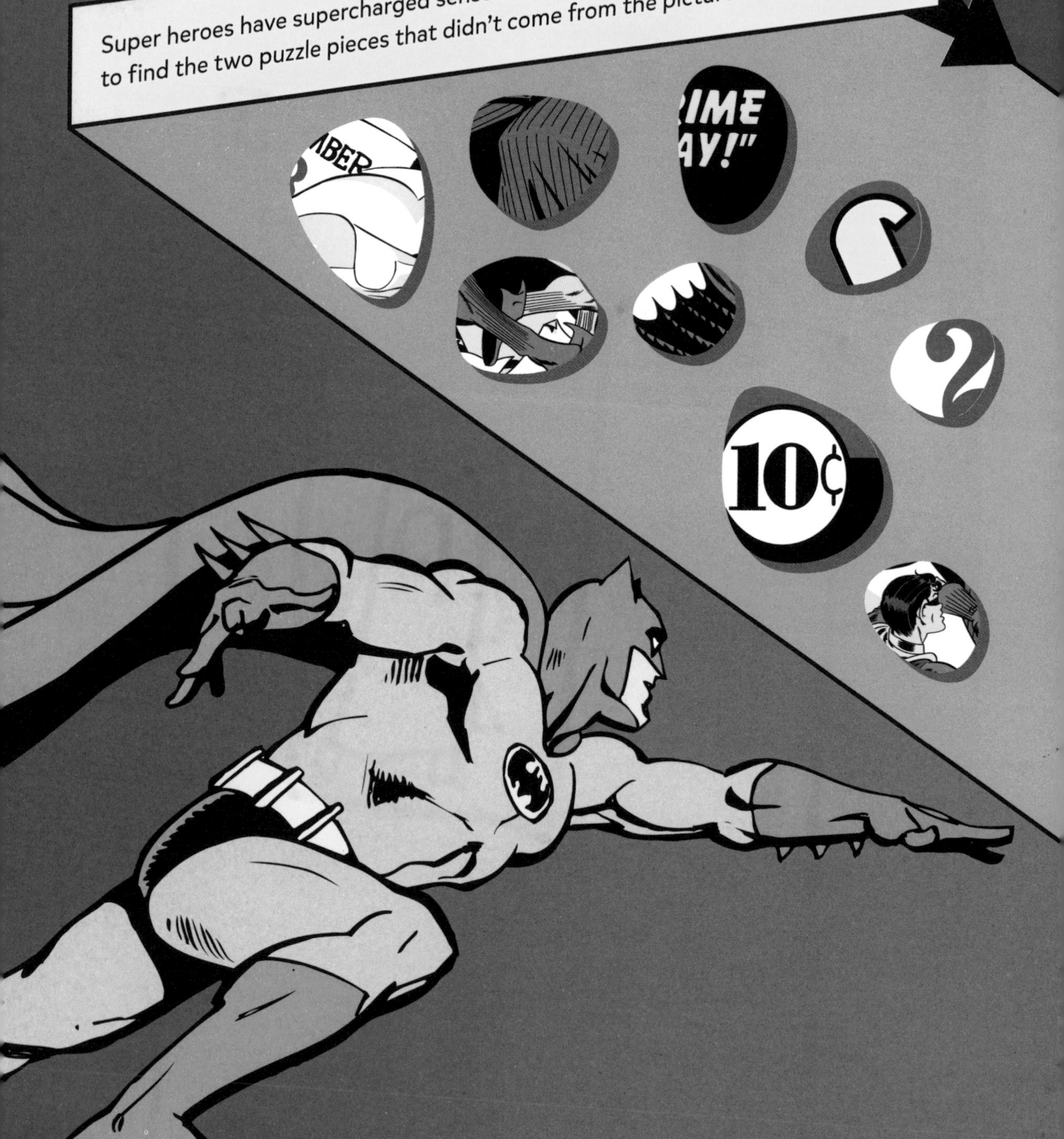

No. 71
Featuring the BOY COMMANDOS
DC COMICS DC ORIGINALS
The BATMAN
Detective
COMICS
JAN.
10¢
BATMAN and ROBIN versus JOKER in "A CRIME A DAY!"
NOVEMBER
27
FRIDAY
EMBER
26
HURSDAY
NOVEMBER
21
SATURD
NOVEMBER
13
NOVEMBER
10
NOVEMBER
1
OVEM
11
NESDAY
ESDAY
BER

Slice It Up!

Katana is a master with any blade. Each of the words below contains three extra letters. Channel your inner samurai and slice out the three unnecessary letters to reveal the name of a super hero or super-villain.

EFROLBIN

SKUPERMTANT

BAMTGPIRSL

LBEXLUTVHOYR

APQJUAMRAN

JWOBKERG

ICYKBORPG

URAJVERN

THWOKFADCE

Archery Adjustment

Green Arrow never misses with his quiver, but something is amiss in one of these images. Find the picture that is different from the others.

The Riddler

The
Winged
Wonders

Frozen Madness!

Don't let this puzzle give you brain freeze! Look closely and you'll find eight items that are amiss.

Pick the Pretender!

One of these Dynamic Duos is a fake! Which pair doesn't belong?

Top That!

Clark Kent is known for wearing classy hats.
But it's time for a change. Give Clark a new look!

Super Hero Showdown!

Green Lantern is strong and disciplined. He never backs down from a challenge. Who is he fighting now? Draw a villain for the Galactic Guardian.

WHAK
WHOOM!
KABOOM!
BOOM

Pattern Play

Bumblebee, Supergirl, Batgirl, and Raven save the day. You can go right, left, up, or down—but not diagonally. Watch out for Harley Quinn!

THE PATTERN

START

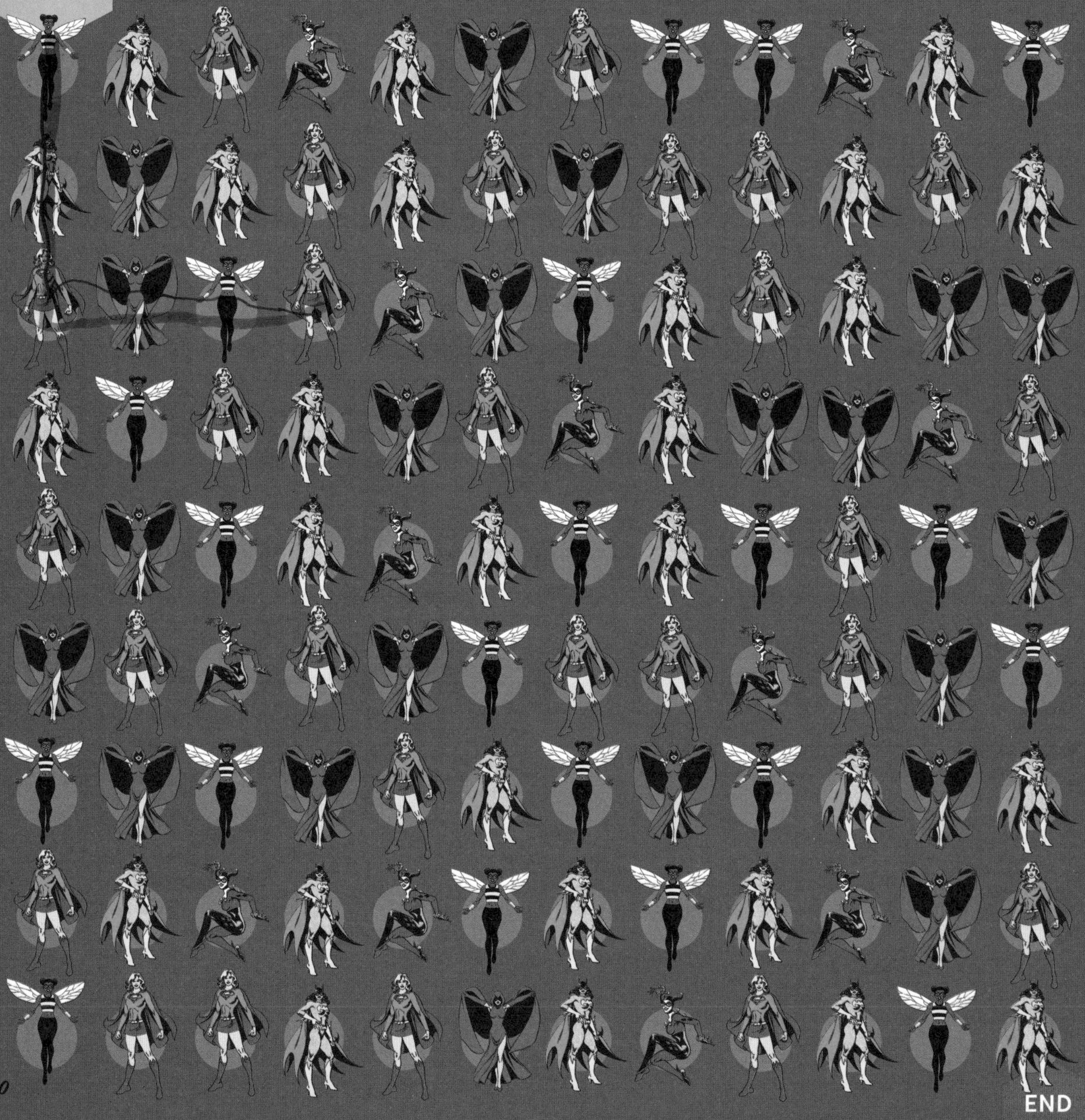

END

Test Your Memory

Study this picture for 30 seconds. Then turn the page and see how many questions you can answer correctly.

Is Your Memory Muddy or Mighty?

Look at the picture on page 81 for 30 seconds and then answer these questions. How many can you get right?

1. WHO IS HOLDING THE WHIP?

a. Wonder Girl
b. Catwoman
c. Raven
d. Harley Quinn

2. WHAT IS SHE WEARING ON HER FEET?

a. Boots
b. Shoes
c. No shoes
d. Clown shoes

3. IS BATMAN CARRYING HIS BATARANG?

a. Yes
b. No

4. HOW MANY CATS ARE IN THE PICTURE?

a. 1
b. 2
c. 3
d. 5

5. WHAT KINDS OF CATS ARE IN THE PICTURE?

a. Tigers
b. Panthers
c. Lions and tigers
d. A lion, a tiger, and a panther

6. WHAT IS BEHIND BATMAN AND ROBIN?

a. A door
b. The side of a tent
c. The bars of a cage
d. Wayne Manor

7. WHICH SHAPE IS ON EACH PEDESTAL?

a. A circle
b. A diamond
c. A crescent moon
d. A star

8. IS ROBIN WEARING A CAPE?

a. Yes
b. No

Mera-Morphosis

Mera rules the seas with Aquaman. She is hot-tempered and powerful. And she possesses the ability to control and manipulate water. She can make tidal waves, rockets, or even creatures out of water. But she can't alter her own shape. Find the image of Mera below that has been changed!

PLASTIC
MAN

Supergirl

Mayhem at Mystery Castle

Something strange is afoot in this spooky castle! See if you can spot seven things that moved or morphed from one picture to the next. Look out behind you—and in front of you!

BATMAN! LOOK OUT! THE KILLER'S HIDING IN THAT SUIT OF ARMOR!

Aim High!

Green Arrow is a master marksman. He has used flame arrows, grenade arrows, flashlight arrows, rain arrows, boxing glove arrows, and arrows carrying fast-drying glue, acid, lassos, and even a buzz saw.

WHAT ARROWS IS HE SHOOTING NOW?

Rearrange the Letters

What words can you spell using just the letters from these characters' names?

EXAMPLE

CLARK KENT

RAN
CAN
TAN
NET
TEAR
KALE
TEN
TANK
TREK
LARK
NEAR
NECK
RAKE
CLEAR
CLEAN
CRANE
TRACK

PLASTIC MAN

SUPERGIRL

SUPERMAN

MARTIAN MANHUNTER

RED TORNADO

GREEN LANTERN

Complete the Creep

Use your sketching skills to finish these sketchy scoundrels.

Find the Fakes

Most of these little shapes are pulled directly from the picture on the right. But three of them don't match. Can you identify the phony fragments?

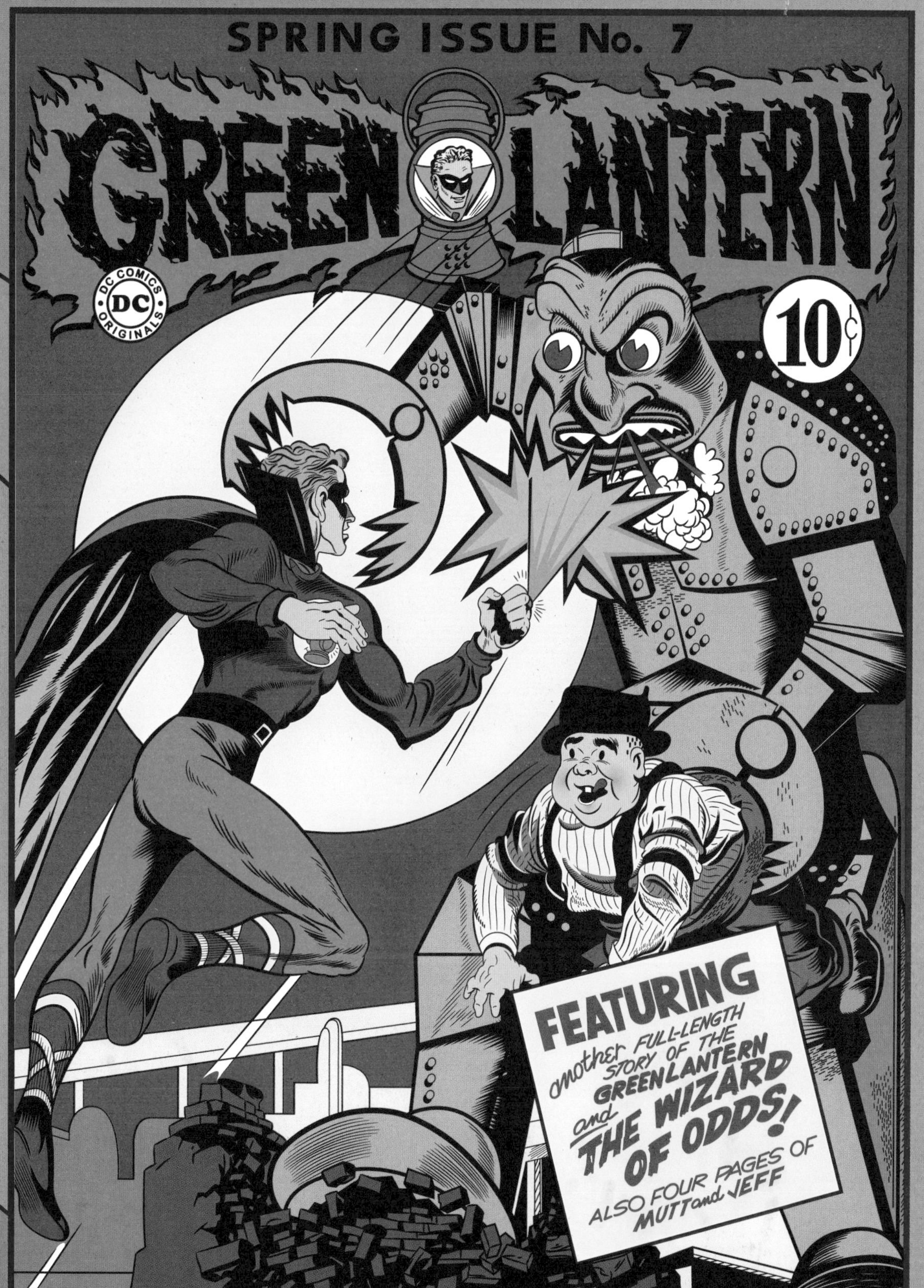
SPRING ISSUE No. 7
GREEN LANTERN
DC COMICS DC ORIGINALS
10¢
FEATURING
another FULL-LENGTH STORY OF THE GREEN LANTERN
and THE WIZARD OF ODDS!
ALSO FOUR PAGES OF MUTT and JEFF

Sound Like a Super Hero

Green Lantern battles a monster, Batman makes a great catch, Superman spots a two-headed lion, Batgirl finds a creepy mask, and Hawkgirl takes on a dragon. What are these heroes thinking and saying?

Oh no!

Robot Terror

Batman battled a giant red robot—and saved the day! The robot has lasers on its head, incredible power, and a plane-crushing grip. Draw your own dangerous robot.

One Superman Is a Sham!

One of the pictures below is not like the rest. Use your enhanced senses to spot the fake.

R
ROBIN
THE TEEN WONDER

Claw-some Kitten Maze

To reach Catwoman, Batman is going to have to work his way through her kitten maze. Which way should he go?

Test Your Memory

Study this picture for 30 seconds. Then turn the page and see how many questions you can answer correctly.

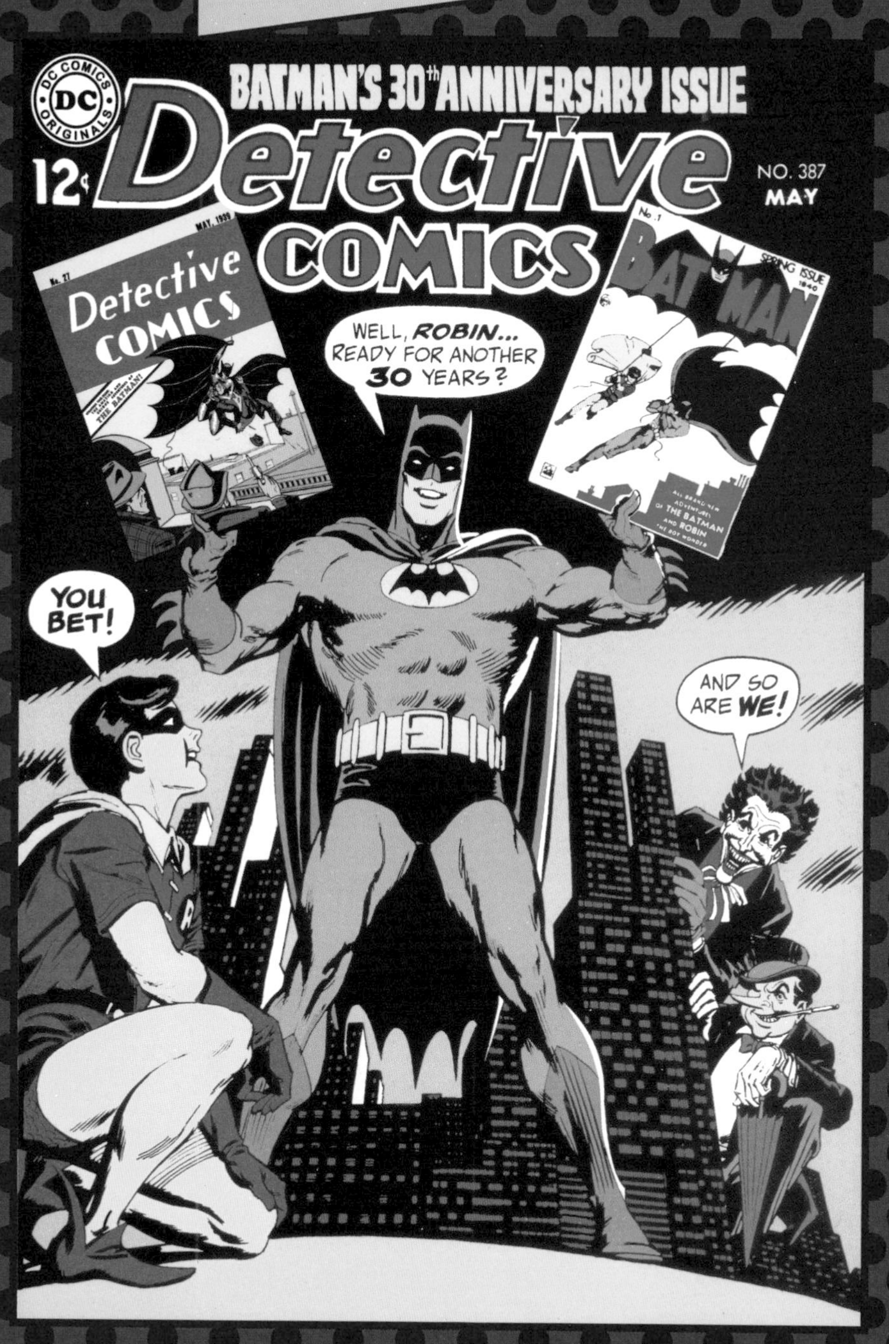

Is Your Memory Fuzzy or Foolproof?

Look at the picture on page 103 for 30 seconds and then answer these questions. How strong are your senses?

1. WHICH SUPER-VILLAINS ARE PEEKING OUT FROM BEHIND THE SKYSCRAPERS?

a. The Joker and the Riddler
b. Harley Quinn and the Joker
c. The Joker and the Penguin
d. Scarecrow and Two-Face

2. WHAT IS ROBIN DOING?

a. Standing
b. Sitting
c. Kneeling
d. A cartwheel

3. HOW MUCH DID THIS COMIC COST?

a. 1¢
b. 12¢
c. 50¢
d. $3

4. WHAT ANNIVERSARY WAS BATMAN CELEBRATING IN THIS COVER?

a. 1st anniversary
b. 25th anniversary
c. 30th anniversary
d. 100th anniversary

5. HOW MANY COMICS IS BATMAN HOLDING UP?

a. 1
b. 2
c. 3
d. 4

6. WHAT COLOR IS BATMAN'S BELT?

a. Yellow
b. Blue
c. Black
d. Purple

Where's Supergirl?

One of these Supergirls is not like the others. Find the imperfect picture.

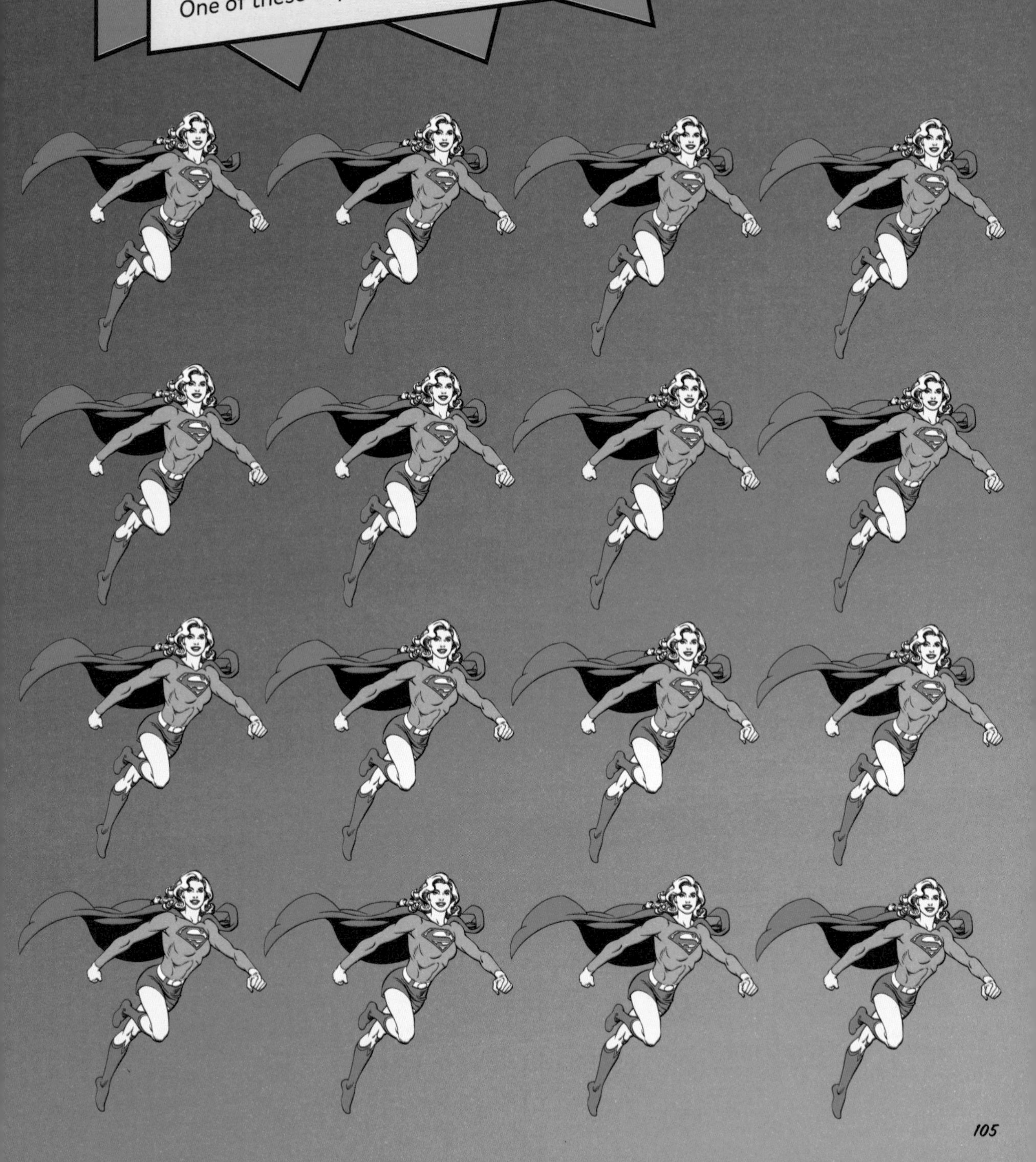

Your Chariot Awaits!

The Batmobile comes with a steel nose for cutting through barriers, a radar screen, searchlights, and a built-in laboratory. What features would you want in your own crime-fighting-mobile. Start drawing . . . NOW!

KNIFE-EDGE STEEL NOSE FOR CUTTING THROUGH BARRIERS
PLASTIC BUBBLE
SEARCHLIGHT THROWS BAT SYMBOL AS WELL AS LIGHT BEAM WHEN DESIRED
RADAR ANTENNAE INSIDE TAIL FIN
TV SCREEN
RADAR SCREEN
ROCKET TUBES
LABORATORY WITH BUILT-IN CABINETS, WORKBENCH, STOOL

What Super-Villain Are You?

STEP 1:

Pick a shape.

STEP 2:

Count the number of points on the shape you chose. Write the number here.

STEP 3:

Start at the top of the next page and begin counting each line. When you reach your number, cross out the words in the line. Then move to the next line and start counting again until you reach your number. Keep counting and crossing out lines. When there is only one option left in each box, circle it. After you have a circled a line, you should no longer count it. When you have one circled line in each box, you are done.

STEP 4:

This is what the boxes tell you:

BOX 1: The first word in your super-villain name

BOX 2: The second word in your super-villain name

BOX 3: The name of your minions

BOX 4: Your strongest superpower

BOX 5: Your fiercest enemy

BOX 6: Your goal

BOX 1:

Demonic

The Grinning

Magnetron

Invisible

Venomous

BOX 2:

Shadowblaster

Spiderhead

Menace

Chessmaster

Undertaker

BOX 3:

The Squinting Squirrels

The Warty Trolls

The Knights of Doom

The Ancient Scrollmakers

The Shape-Shifting Skunkpeople

BOX 4:

Silent communication with monkeys

Changing the world from night to day by sneezing

Ability to balance anything on your head

Fastest skateboarder on Earth

Shooting pineapple juice from your eyes

BOX 5:

Green Lantern

Superman

Cyborg

The Flash

Wonder Woman

BOX 6:

To plunge the world into darkness

To own all the jelly beans in the world

To control all technology with magnets

To get an automatic A++ on all homework forever

To be able to control all TVs worldwide

Power Lifter

Sometimes Superman lifts more than people's spirits when he saves the day. He can lift a bus, a house, or even a whole school with everyone still inside. What is he carrying now?

Power Punch!

Some puzzle pieces shook loose! Each loose piece has a letter. Write the letters in the spots where the pieces belong.

AQUAMAN

The FLASH

Rainbow Change-up

This not-so-Dark Knight has been changing up his costume. What else has changed from the first picture to the second? Find nine changes.

Featuring "The Rainbow Batman!"
BUT, BATMAN, LAST NIGHT YOU WORE THE GREEN COSTUME -- AND TONIGHT YOU'RE WEARING THE RED! WHY?
I MUST, ROBIN-- I MUST WEAR A DIFFERENT-COLORED BATMAN COSTUME EACH NIGHT!

Brilliant Batarangs

Batman invented ingenious tools and gadgets. His Batarangs could carry bombs, magnets, ropes, flashing lights, cameras, and more. Invent your own amazing Batarang.

POLICE WHISTLE BATARANG

ROPE BATARANG

FLASHBULB BATARANG

BOMB BATARANG

SEEING-EYE BATARANG

MAGNET BATARANG

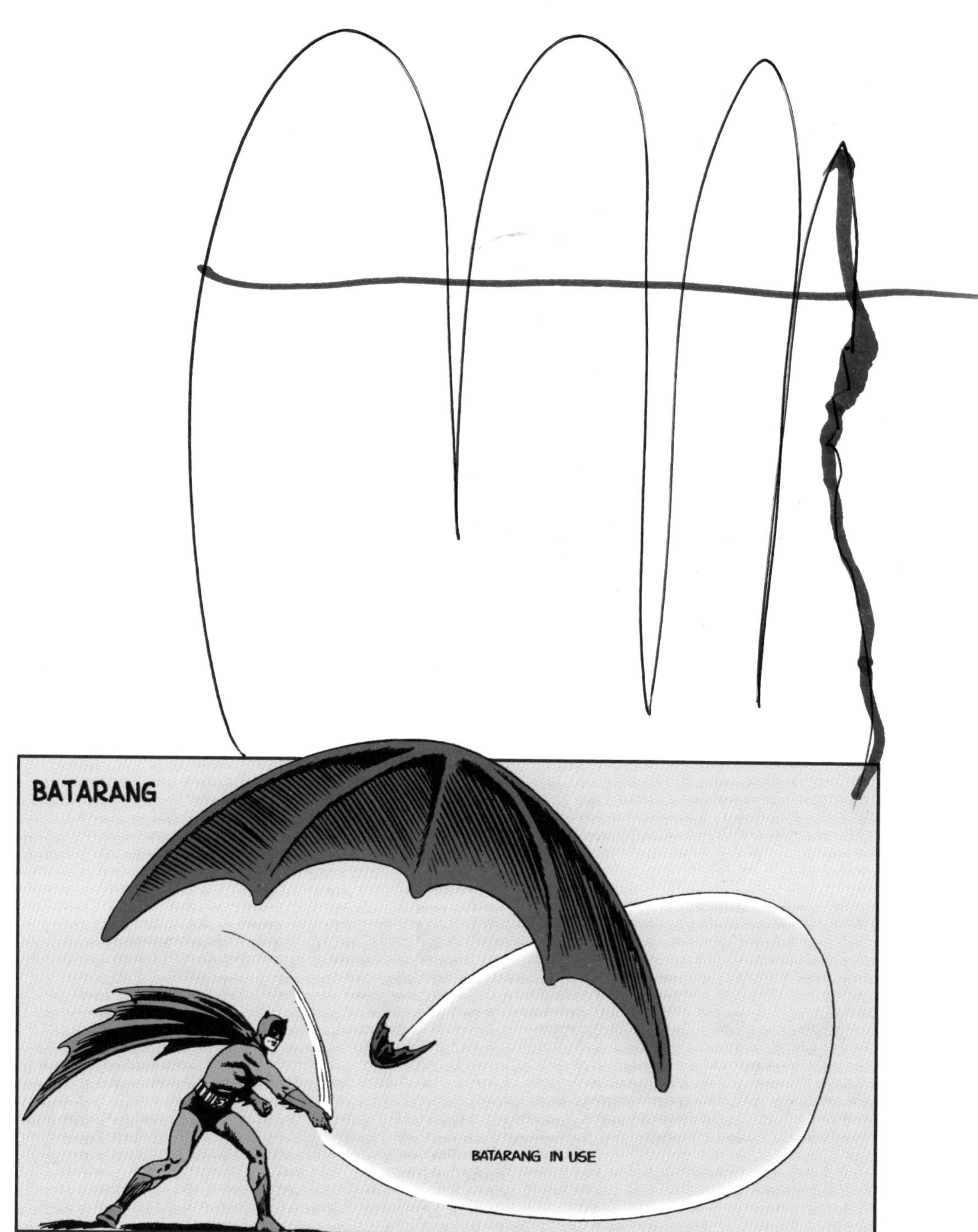
BATARANG
BATARANG IN USE

Underwater Menace

Aquaman has battled all sorts of baddies, including a mutant talking shark, murderous fish gods, and underwater fire trolls. What underwater monster is he after now?

Power Play

The Flash is the Fastest Man Alive. If you were that quick, how would you use your powers of super-speed?

After experimenting with star matter, physicist Ray Palmer became the Atom. He can shrink down to be smaller than a wedding ring—or even shrink to subatomic levels. He can hide inside a person's ear, surf on someone's blood stream, and sneak through phone lines. What would you do with shrinking powers?

Hawkman and Hawkgirl have giant wings. With the help of a special element called Nth Metal, they can fly. Nth Metal also gives them super-strength and healing powers. What would you do if you got your hands on some Nth Metal?

Wonder Woman's incredible, unbreakable Golden Lasso of Truth compels people to tell the truth. Imagine you had something that would make everyone totally honest. How would you use it? What would you call it?

BATGIRL

High-Octane Brainpower

With genius-level intellect and master martial arts skills, Batgirl is an unstoppable force for good. Use your brainpower to solve this puzzle about her.

R	O	W	B	S	I	N	F	E	C	S	K	E	A	O
E	G	A	S	L	E	A	Q	Z	O	Y	V	O	M	S
H	O	Y	A	O	G	E	U	T	I	R	G	A	I	T
I	T	O	C	S	A	P	R	E	A	X	A	E	S	R
E	H	B	L	A	C	K	B	E	L	T	S	C	H	A
X	A	K	E	I	E	Y	S	I	K	Z	R	M	L	T
O	M	O	V	N	A	D	B	L	D	C	K	N	I	E
T	Q	S	E	O	B	R	I	P	A	T	A	L	B	G
R	O	E	R	U	A	F	A	O	G	E	S	H	A	Y
E	I	L	F	R	L	S	Y	H	S	T	E	U	T	B
Y	A	Z	I	H	W	R	E	T	U	P	M	O	C	E
S	B	A	G	O	D	Q	U	N	W	L	R	I	Y	P
L	N	E	C	I	T	S	U	J	B	E	I	O	C	W
E	O	J	U	J	I	T	S	U	A	O	G	F	L	Y
N	E	Z	S	O	F	E	V	I	T	C	E	T	E	D

All of the words in the word list can be found in the puzzle on the left. They can go up, down, forward, backward, and even diagonally.

Word List

BATCYCLE
BLACK BELT
CLEVER
COMPUTER WHIZ
DETECTIVE
GOTHAM
HACKER
JUJITSU
JUSTICE
LIBRARIAN
ORACLE
STRATEGY

Jigsaw Jokermobile

It seems like Jokers are everywhere in this puzzle. But the sinister scene is hard to see with so many missing pieces. Match the pieces to their place in the puzzle.

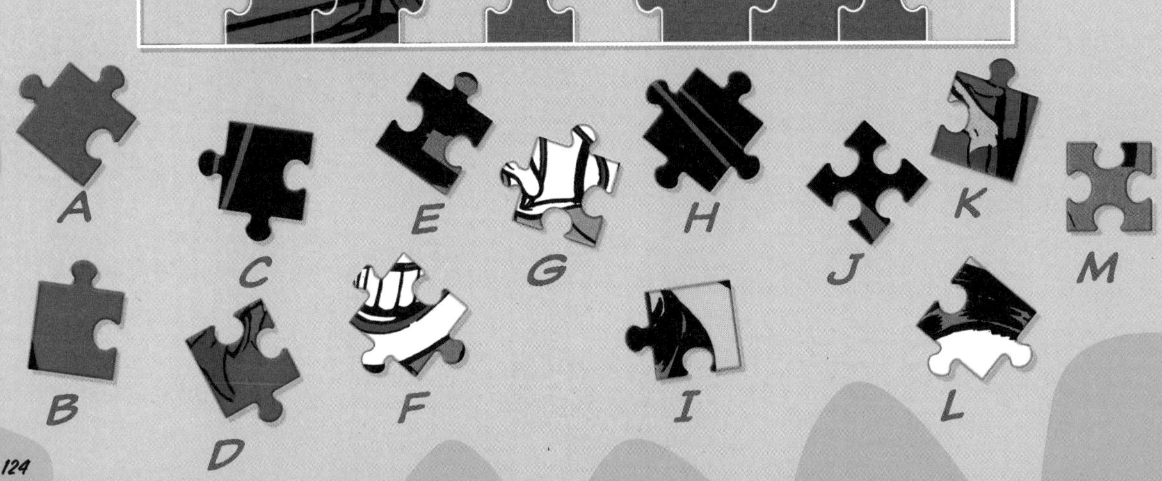

Hot Pursuit

Wonder Woman, Aquaman, and Cyborg are hot on the trail of Darkseid. They must navigate the maze and avoid the burning fire pits. Only one path will lead through the treacherous terrain. Which super hero will confront this evildoer?

HARLEY
QUINN

GREEN LANTERN

Shadow Matcher

JUSTICE LEAGUE of AMERICA

The Justice League has tracked a super-villain to a realm of shadows, but they need to be able to spot one another. Can you help? Match these super heroes to their warped shadows to earn your temporary membership to this group of extraordinary crime fighters.

Name That Hero!

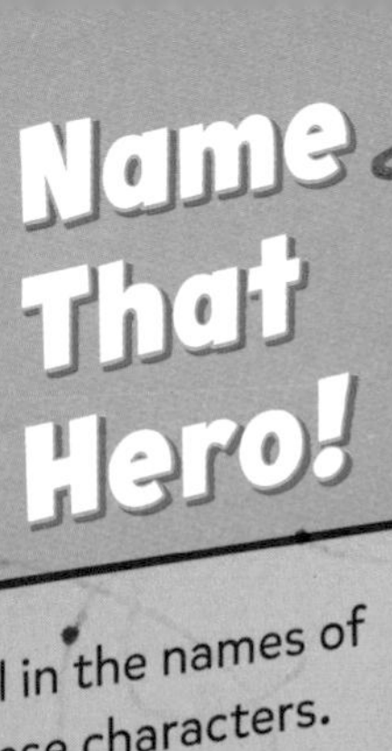

Fill in the names of these characters. Write the letters on the blanks next to each picture. Put the letters in the red boxes on the blue lines below. Then unscramble the letters to reveal the name of a super-villain who has been causing trouble in Gotham City.

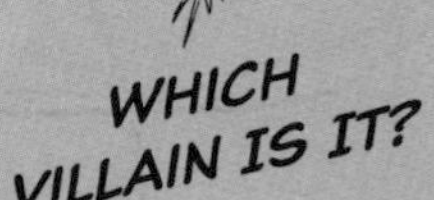

UNSCRAMBLED SUPER-VILLAIN NAME HERE

Tricky Tracks

The Riddler is up to his old tricks. He's tangled up all the pathways so no one can figure out which way to go. Follow each pathway to see where each super hero ends up.

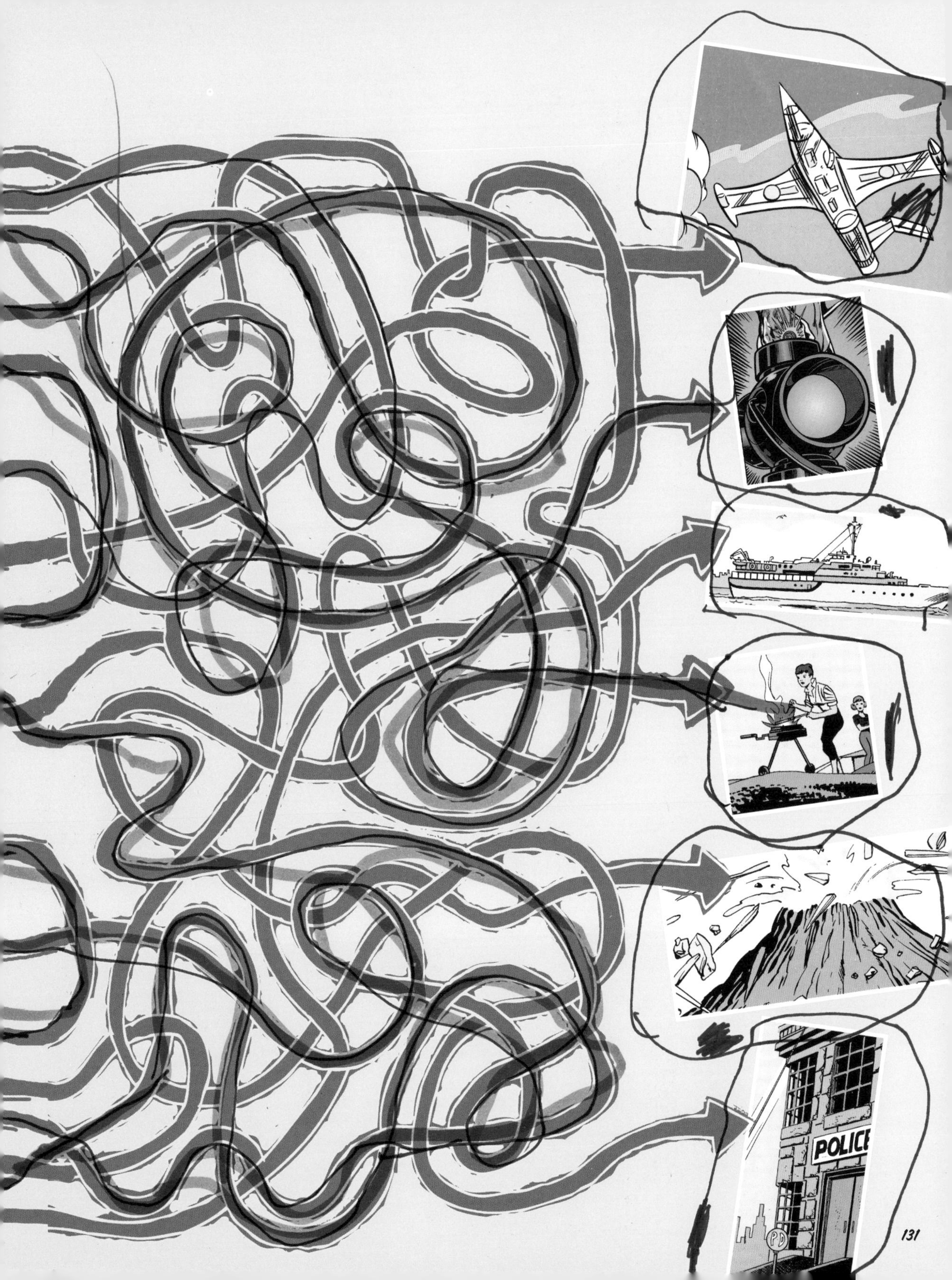
POLICE
PD

Shine On!
When the Bat-Signal appears in the air, Batman knows there's trouble afoot. What would your signal look like?
TM
R

Beach Brainteasers

Use the key below to decode each of the letters and uncover the answers.

HOW DID AQUAMAN LEARN TO READ AND WRITE?

HOW IS AQUAMAN LIKE THE NEW KID AT SCHOOL?

WHY IS AQUAMAN A TERRIBLE GOLFER?

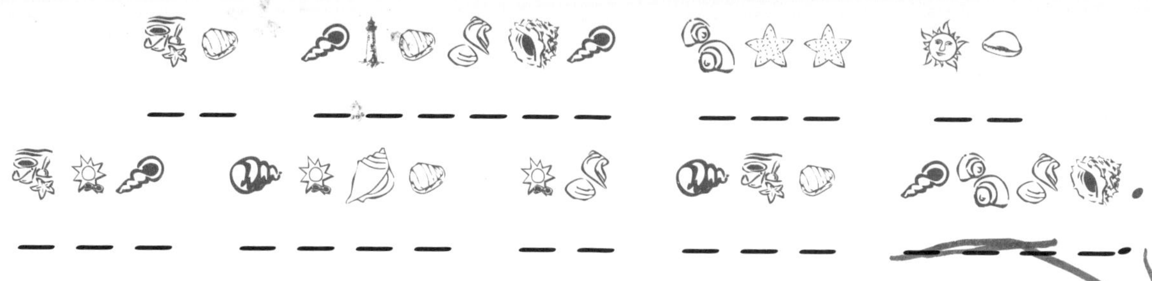

Buzz-y Buzz-y Bee Maze
Bumblebee can shrink down small enough to fly through this maze. She can locate the stolen diamond in the center and then fly out of the exit. Show her the way!
EXIT

Bendable Beyond Belief

Plastic Man can twist, bend, and stretch into the craziest shapes. What's the wackiest position you can think of?

Man of Steel Matching Game

Rearrange the letters in the first column. Then draw a line to the matching word in the middle. Match the words in the middle to their descriptions on the right.

POTNYKR	HEAT VISION	A twisted clone of Superman whose sense of right and wrong is all mixed up
CSUTJIE	ROCKET	The S on Superman's chest
SLOTMROEIP	BIZARRO	A superpower that really warms things up
KEOCTR	KRYPTON	A superpower that helps Superman get places fast
OPRRTREE	FLIGHT	This is how Superman got to Earth
MYBSLO	REPORTER	Superman fights for truth, _______, and the American Way
THEA IONSIV	SYMBOL	The city where Superman lives
RZIBOAR	BRAINIAC	Superman's home planet
CBINIRAA	JUSTICE	Incredibly smart super-villain who likes to capture cities, shrink them, and trap them in bottles
GTIFLH	METROPOLIS	Clark Kent's job at the *Daily Planet*

Pinwheel Puzzle-O-Rama
Do you have super-sight? Can you match these characters to their swirly clones?

Use Your X-ray Vision

Superman has tracked the bad guys to this abandoned building. He uses his X-ray vision to look inside. What does he see? Write or draw your answer.

Bananas

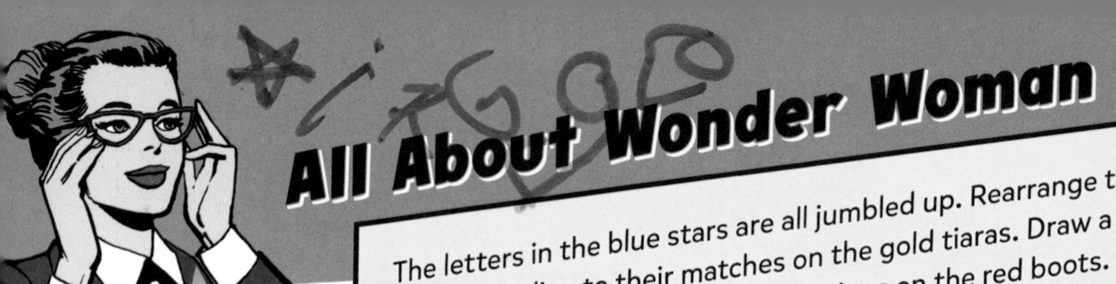

All About Wonder Woman

The letters in the blue stars are all jumbled up. Rearrange them and draw a line to their matches on the gold tiaras. Draw a line to match the words to their descriptions on the red boots.

APHILPOTY

LARTCEEBS

SNOZAAM

THEACHE

OASLS

IDNAA IRPCNE

MUJAP

ESRIPNCS

AATIGGN

ARTIA

PRINCESS

AMAZONS

BRACELETS

GIGANTA

TIARA

HIPPOLYTA

LASSO

CHEETAH

JUMPA

DIANA PRINCE

Because her mother is a queen,
Wonder Woman is a ________.

A giant kangaroo who sometimes helps Wonder Woman fight crime

A super-villain who can turn into a dangerous cat with superhuman strength, speed, and agility

An enemy of Wonder Woman who can grow to be hundreds of feet tall in just a few seconds. She's big trouble!

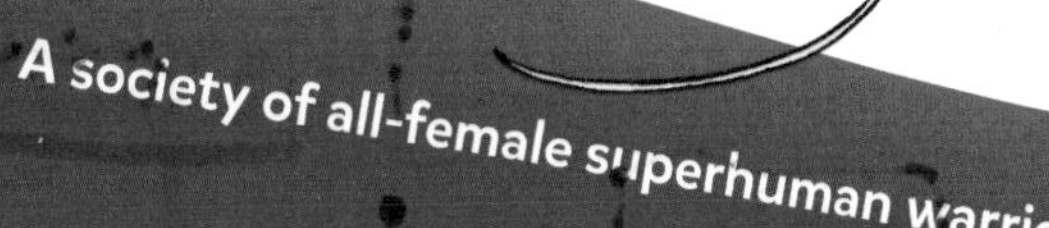

A society of all-female superhuman warriors

A beautiful band with razor-sharp edges that Wonder Woman wears on her head. It's both jewelry and a weapon!

Wonder Woman wears these indestructible cuffs. They are so strong they can even deflect bullets.

Wonder Woman's mother, the queen of the Amazons

The name Wonder Woman uses when she assumes her secret identity

When Wonder Woman captures criminals with this tool, they have to tell the truth.

Harley's Challenge

Leave it to Harley Quinn to devise a difficult maze. Can you make it through?

What Makes a Hero?

Super heroes have many traits in common. They are smart, helpful, and strong. Find more heroic words below. The words can go up, down, forward, backward, and even diagonally.

WORD LIST

ALERT	COURAGEOUS	POWERFUL
BOLD	FEARLESS	SELFLESS
BRAVE	GUTSY	SKILLED
CARING	HONEST	SPEEDY
CLEVER	KIND	TRUSTWORTHY

O	R	S	T	A	O	R	C	H	U	R	W	S	N	A
R	E	E	C	B	C	U	H	O	F	A	Y	K	O	J
I	V	S	E	A	O	S	A	L	E	S	S	I	B	A
H	E	R	U	N	U	D	Y	A	J	A	S	L	P	O
T	L	H	D	B	E	E	L	C	A	O	Z	L	U	X
P	C	O	U	R	A	G	E	O	U	S	O	E	N	G
O	W	N	C	A	I	N	S	D	B	E	A	D	L	N
W	F	E	P	V	W	H	E	S	V	L	Q	U	A	I
E	V	S	P	E	E	D	Y	A	E	F	E	X	U	R
R	U	T	G	G	Z	U	B	S	P	L	D	R	Y	A
F	S	Y	S	T	U	G	A	O	A	E	R	U	T	C
U	K	E	B	B	R	A	N	M	U	S	D	A	R	O
L	I	K	I	A	B	E	J	K	L	S	E	S	E	S
O	B	A	J	K	I	N	D	O	H	O	N	A	L	F
E	Y	H	T	R	O	W	T	S	U	R	T	C	A	L

Crime-Fighting Crossword

Read the clues below. Then write the answers in the crossword puzzle on the right.

ACROSS

1. This samurai super heroine is skilled with a sword.
3. Black ________ is a super heroine who fights crime with her sonic scream and martial arts skills.
7. This super hero is just one of an intergalactic group of crime fighters who can create whatever they want using pure energy.
8. Aquaman once saved a city from a huge tidal ________ by using his powers to calm the rough water.
9. Superman has a yellow *S* symbol on his long, red ________.
13. Superman's cousin ________ is also known as Kara Zor-El.
15. ________ Lane is a reporter for the *Daily Planet*. She's always on call for a good Superman story.
16. Green Lantern must recharge his power ________ to use his superpowers.
17. Batman creates new body armor, gadgets, and inventions in his secret laboratory known as the ________.

DOWN

1. This mineral from Superman's home planet drains his strength and makes him weak.
2. This smarty-pants scientist super hero can shrink down to microscopic sizes.
4. The Dynamic Duo is made up of Batman and ________.
5. Superman's secret Arctic hideaway is the ________ of Solitude.
6. Commissioner Gordon runs the police department in Batman's home, ________ City.
9. When she is not prowling around the rooftops, this sneaky burglar likes to toy with Batman.
10. Star City is the hometown of the extraordinary archer, Green ________.
11. Superman is a super hero. Two-Face is a ________.
12. Bruce Wayne, a.k.a. Batman, often gets help from his skilled and loyal butler, ________.
14. The Bat-________ projects the Bat Symbol into the sky.

™

WORD LIST
Alfred
Arrow
Atom
Batcave
Canary
Cape
Catwoman
Fortress
Gotham
Green Lantern
Katana
Kryptonite
Lois
Ring
Robin
Signal
Supergirl
Villain
Wave
1
2
3
4
5
6
7
8
9
10
11
12
13
14
15
16
17

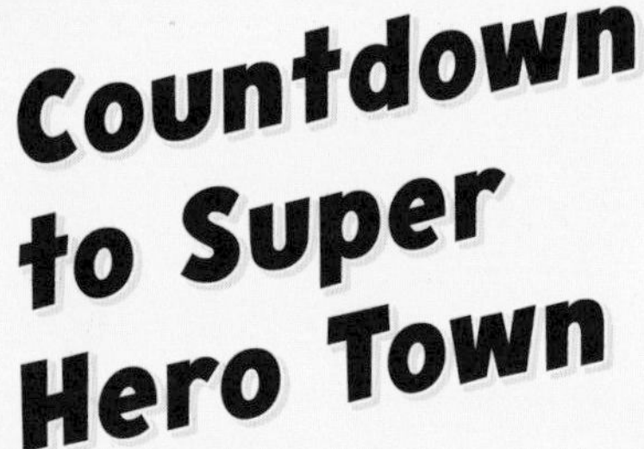

STEP 1:

Pick a shape.

STEP 2:

Count the number of points on the shape you chose. Write the number here.

STEP 3:

Start at the top of the next page and begin counting each line. When you reach your number, cross out the words in the line. Then move to the next line and start counting again until you reach your number. Keep counting and crossing out lines. When there is only one option left in each box, circle it. After you have a circled a line, you should no longer count it. When you have one circled line in each box, you are done.

STEP 4:

This is what the boxes tell you:

BOX 1: How you got your superpowers

BOX 2: Your strongest superpower

BOX 3: Your most heightened super sense

BOX 4: The first word in your super hero name

BOX 5: The second word in your super hero name

BOX 6: The thing that causes you to lose your powers

BOX 7: Your fiercest enemy

BOX 8: The name of your secret hideout

BOX 1:

Bitten by a fanged werekitten
Exposed to toxic ice cream
Born on a faraway nose-shaped planet
Raised by a tribe of talking amoebas
Stepped on by the ancient Greek goddess of flatulence

BOX 2:

Super-speed on Tuesdays
Ability to communicate with gerbils
Super-strength from 3 to 6 a.m.
Power of hummingbird flight
Incredible belching skills

BOX 3:

Can smell popcorn five miles away
Can hear the flapping of ladybug wings
Can see through lampposts
Can hear what trees are thinking
Can smell when people are grumpy

BOX 4:

Purple Polka-Dotted
Shark
Whispering
Satin
Sneezing

BOX 5:

Arrow
Thunder
Dolphin
Warrior
Speedster

BOX 6:

Skateboards
Butterflies
Librarian shushes
Chocolate cupcakes
Mirrored sunglasses

BOX 7:

The Evil Dragonfly
The Upset Pteradactyl
The Red Ravioli Maker
The Wicked Knitting Knight
The Scarlet Gym Teacher

BOX 8:

The Homework Hideaway
The Subterranean Soccer Cave
Raccoon's Revenge
The Dentist's Chair Lounge
Tree House of Anxiety

Green Arrow to the Rescue!

Can Green Arrow save the day? You bet he can. Can you solve this puzzle? You bet you can too! Just find nine things that have changed from the first picture to the second.

THERE'S ONLY ONE WAY TO FREE THE JUSTICE LEAGUE MEMBERS IMPRISONED INSIDE THAT DIAMOND-SPLIT IT IN TWO WITH THIS DIAMOND-TIPPED ARROW!
HERE IT IS-- THE STORY YOU'VE BEEN WAITING FOR...!
GREEN ARROW JOINS THE JUSTICE LEAGUE of AMERICA
"DOOM of the STAR DIAMOND!"

Answers

p. 4 Dragon Race!

Superman

p. 8 Robot Remodeling

p. 11 Code-Breaking with Batman

The note says:

Harley,

Meet me at the hideout at noon. Bring your mallet. I will bring my happy gas. And we will hit the town!

p. 14 Once a Trickster, Always a Trickster

p. 16 Is Your Memory Shipshape or Shoddy?

1. **c.** Pink
2. **c.** 4
3. **b.** Yes, a dog.
4. **b.** Trees and a lake
5. **d.** A surfboard
6. **a.** Waving his hand

p. 18 Operation Rescue Lois

p. 19 Justice League Jigsaw

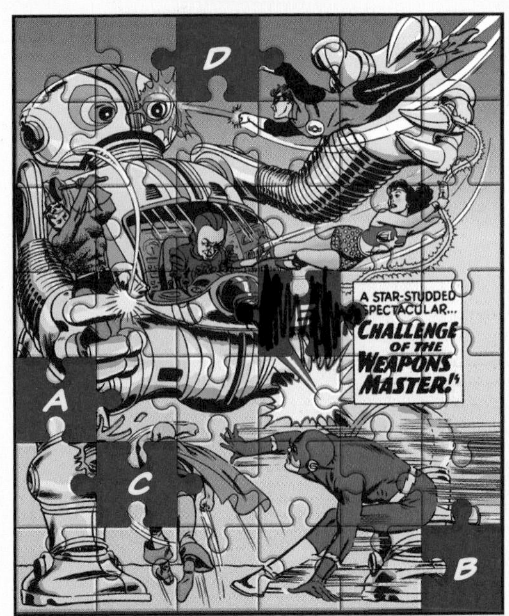

p. 25 Scan It Like Cyborg

T	E	C	H	N	O	L	O	G	Y	A	F	S	U	L
A	X	G	U	K	M	V	E	E	N	I	H	C	A	M
F	P	U	D	I	C	O	A	O	I	C	Z	A	E	O
R	E	D	E	Y	E	N	E	S	Y	I	Q	E	N	T
E	R	E	I	R	E	L	S	W	J	T	U	P	O	I
K	I	I	O	V	F	S	U	G	C	E	C	B	T	O
F	M	K	A	Y	S	V	I	C	D	N	O	I	S	N
Y	E		D	L	G	E	N	R	Y	R	V	S	R	S
S	N	A	T	I	T	N	E	E	T	E	J	T	O	E
X	T	R	V	A	E	J	G	W	E	B	A	A	T	N
I	U	M	E	Q	S	O	U	E	B	Y	K	R	C	S
F	C	O	M	P	U	T	E	R	F	C	Z	F	I	O
A	I	R	S	U	G	V	O	U	I	K	A	I	V	R
S	U	P	E	R	H	U	M	A	N	X	L	R	O	S
J	U	S	T	I	C	E	L	E	A	G	U	E	D	F

p. 28 One Too Many

This piece doesn't belong:

p. 32 Use Your Eagle Eyes

p. 33 Shadow People

p. 34 Journey to the Joker

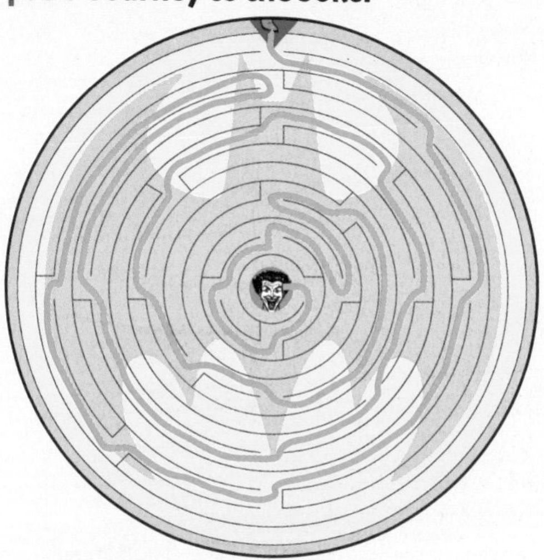

p. 36 Follow the Pattern

p. 37 Machine Meltdown!

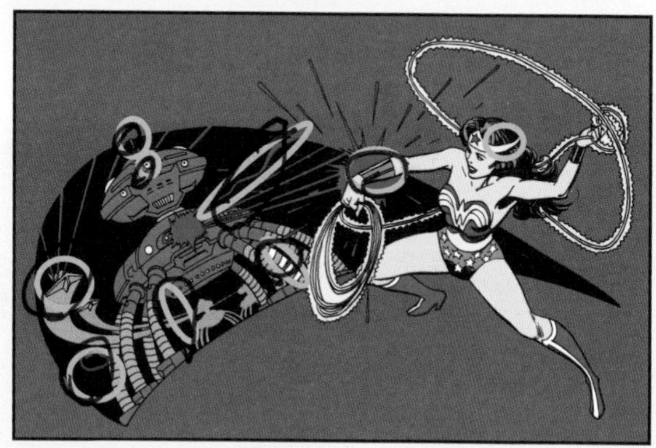

p. 38 Catch That Bird!

The Flash captures the Penguin.

p. 40 Shape-Shifters

p. 41 After Them!

p. 45 Zatanna's Magic Jumble

TWIHC = Witch
RAMCH = Charm
SLELP = Spell
RKICT = Trick
NATCH = Chant
RADYZWIR = Wizardry
CABRAADABAR = Abracadabra
OCHUPSCOUS = Hocus Pocus
CYROSER = Sorcery
SLINOUIL = Illusion

p. 48 Crossword Caper

p. 50 Great Green Scramble

Brightest

p. 52 Batman and Robin

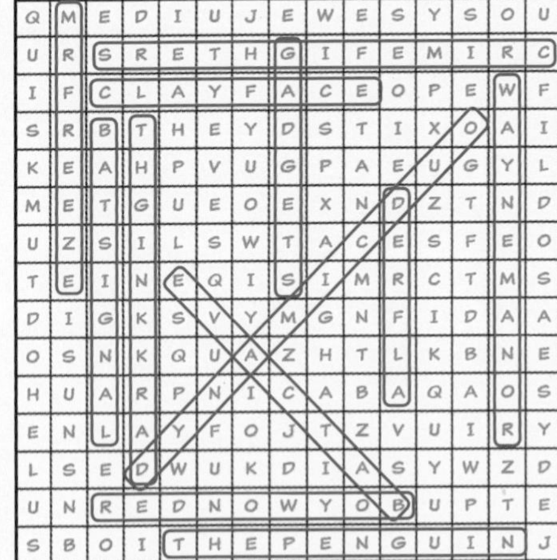

p. 53 Riddler's Labyrinth

Zatanna

p. 56 Decode the Jokes!

The Lasso from El Paso
Spyborg
Ice scream
A good night's work
She doesn't use short cuts.

p. 60 Beware of the Crocs!

p. 64 Time to Recharge!

p. 65 Windblown Balderdash

URFWLEOP = Powerful
ITHYGM = Mighty
ETATRIGCS = Strategic
RAMST = Smart
ICEDTADED = Dedicated
GROUACEOUS = Courageous
REABV = Brave
DREARPEP = Prepared
OALLY = Loyal
ENIDFOCNT = Confident
EPLAPBOTSUN = Unstoppable

p. 68 Mismatched Pieces

These two pieces do not belong:  

p. 70 Slice It Up!

EFROLBIN = Robin
JWOBKERG = Joker
SKUPERMTANT = Superman
ICYKBORRG = Cyborg
BAMTGRIRSL = Batgirl
URAJVERN = Raven
LBEXLUTVHOYR = Lex Luthor
THWOKFADCE = Two-Face
ARQJUAMRAN = Aquaman

p. 71 Archery Adjustment

There is an extra arrow stuck in the center of the target.

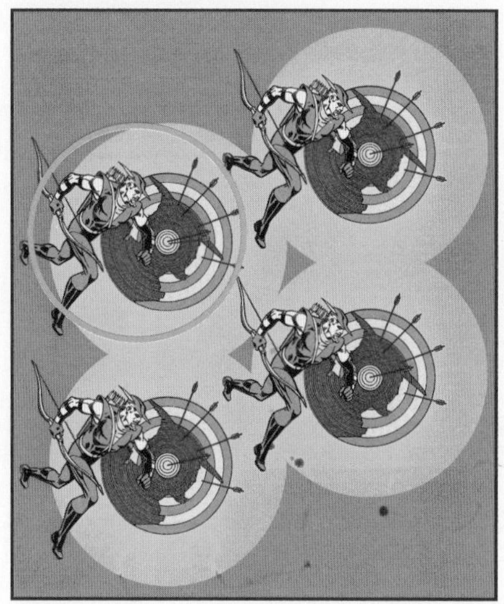

p. 74 Frozen Madness!

p. 76 Pick the Pretender!

Batman's glove has gotten smoother.

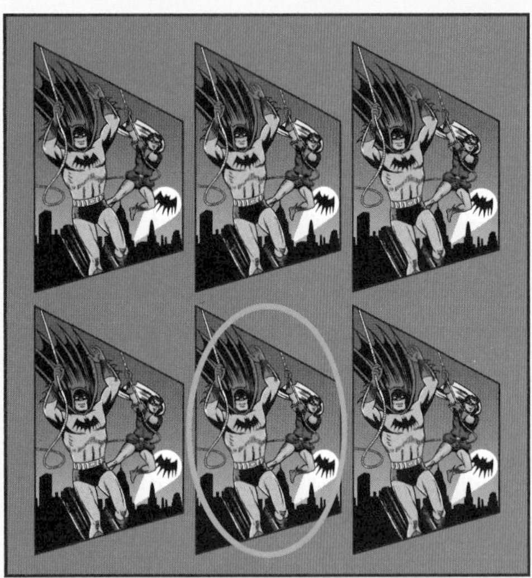

p. 80 Pattern Play

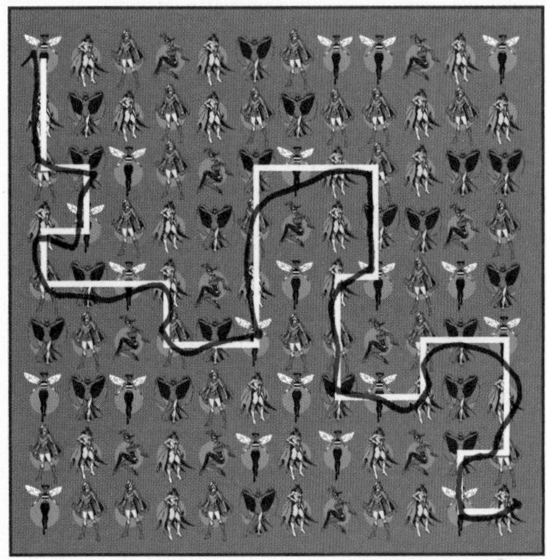

p. 82 Is Your Memory Muddy or Mighty?

1. **b.** Catwoman
2. **a.** Boots
3. **b.** No
4. **c.** 3
5. **d.** A lion, a tiger, and a panther
6. **c.** The bars of a cage
7. **d.** A star
8. **a.** Yes

p. 83 Mera-Morphosis

One of Mera's flippers has shrunk!

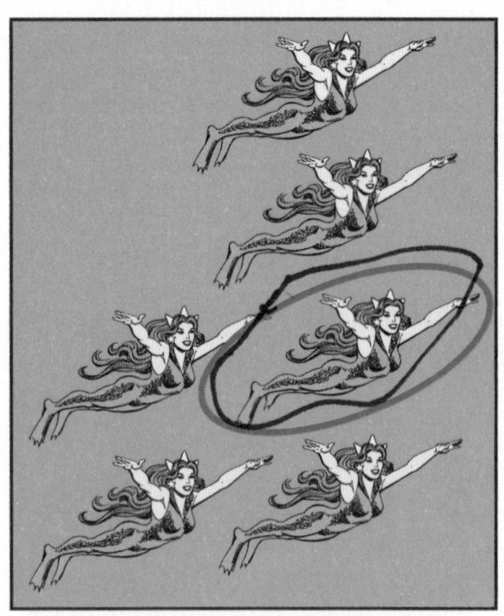

p. 86 Mayhem at Mystery Castle

p. 94 Find the Fakes

These pieces don't belong: 

p. 99 One Superman Is a Sham!

Clark Kent's glasses have lost an arm.

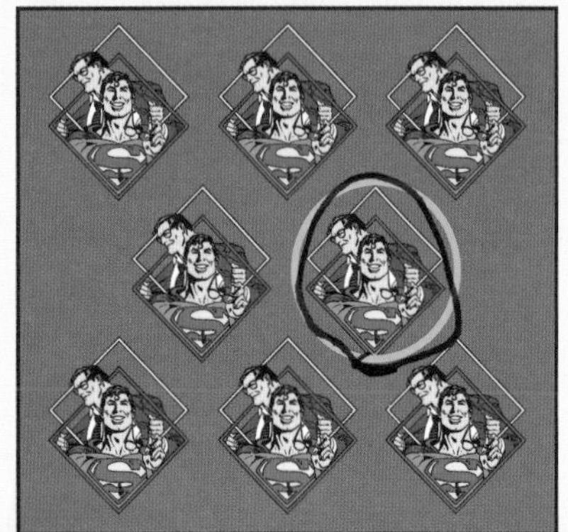

p. 102 Claw-some Kitten Maze

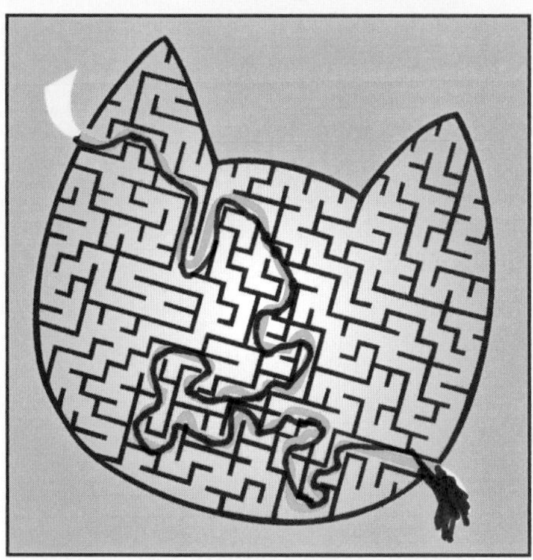

p. 104 Is Your Memory Fuzzy or Foolproof?

1. **c.** The Joker and the Penguin
2. **c.** Kneeling
3. **b.** 12¢
4. **c.** 30th anniversary
5. **b.** 2
6. **a.** Yellow

p. 105 Where's Supergirl?

Supergirl's cape has been trimmed.

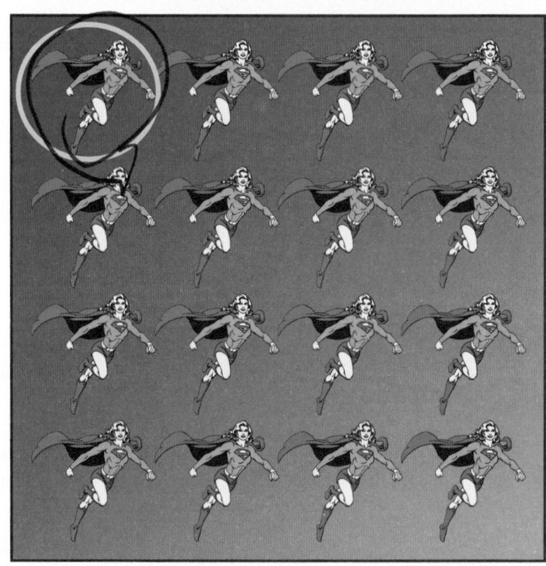

p. 111 Power Punch!

p. 114 Rainbow Change-up

p. 123 High-Octane Brainpower

R	O	W	B	S	I	N	F	E	C	S	K	E	A	O
E	G	A	S	L	E	A	Q	Z	O	Y	V	O	M	S
H	O	Y	A	O	G	E	U	T	I	R	G	A	I	T
I	T	O	C	S	A	P	R	E	A	X	A	E	S	R
E	H	B	L	A	C	K	B	E	L	T	S	C	H	A
X	A	K	E	I	E	Y	S	I	K	Z	R	M	L	T
O	M	O	V	N	A	D	B	L	D	C	K	N	I	E
T	Q	S	E	O	B	R	I	P	A	T	A	L	B	G
R	O	E	R	U	A	F	A	O	G	E	S	H	A	Y
E	I	L	F	R	L	S	Y	H	S	T	E	U	T	B
Y	A	Z	I	H	W	R	E	T	U	P	M	O	C	E
S	B	A	G	O	D	Q	U	N	W	L	R	I	Y	P
L	N	E	C	I	T	S	U	J	B	E	I	O	C	W
E	O	J	U	J	I	T	S	U	A	O	G	F	L	Y
N	E	Z	S	O	F	E	V	I	T	C	E	T	E	D

p. 124 Jigsaw Jokermobile

p. 125 Hot Pursuit

Wonder Woman

p. 128 Shadow Matcher

p. 129 Name That Hero!

Hawkgirl
Batman
Aquaman
Superman
Cyborg
Robin
Katana
Supergirl
Green Lantern
Wonder Woman
Answer: The Penguin

p. 130 Tricky Tracks

Superman ends up at a barbecue.
Wonder Woman ends up at the Power Battery.
Black Canary ends up on a boat.
Green Lantern ends up at a volcano.
Martian Manhunter and Bumblebee end up together.

p. 134 Beach Brainteasers

He spelled with seashells by the seashore.
Sometimes they both feel like fish out of water.
He spends all of his time in the sand.

p. 136 Buzz-y Buzz-y Bee Maze

p. 138 Man of Steel Matching Game

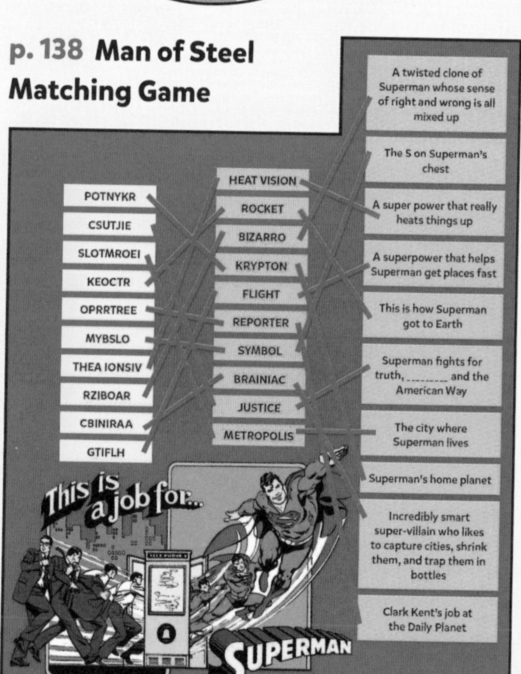

p. 139 Pinwheel Puzzle-O-Rama

p. 142 All About Wonder Woman

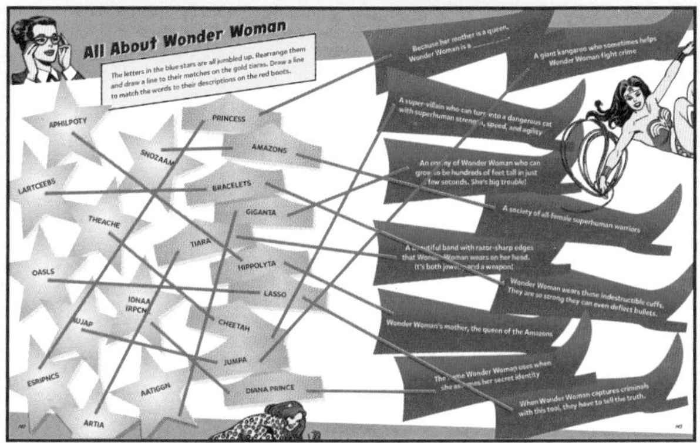

p. 144 Harley's Challenge

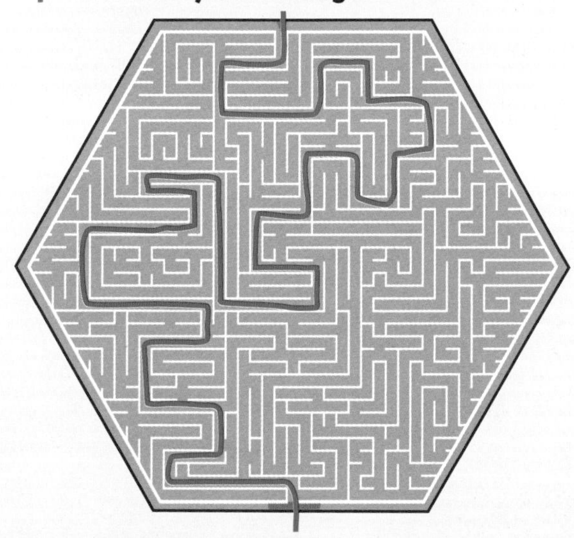

p. 145 What Makes a Hero?

O	R	S	T	A	O	R	C	H	U	R	W	S	N	A
R	E	E	C	B	C	U	H	O	F	A	Y	K	O	J
I	V	S	E	A	O	S	A	L	E	S	S	I	B	A
H	E	R	U	N	U	D	Y	A	J	A	S	L	P	O
T	L	H	D	B	E	E	L	C	A	O	Z	L	U	X
P	C	O	U	R	A	G	E	O	U	S	O	E	N	G
O	W	N	C	A	I	N	S	D	B	E	A	D	L	N
W	F	E	P	V	W	H	E	S	V	L	Q	U	A	I
E	V	S	P	E	E	D	Y	A	E	F	E	X	U	R
R	U	T	G	G	Z	U	B	S	P	L	D	R	Y	A
F	S	Y	S	T	U	G	A	O	A	E	R	U	T	C
U	K	E	B	B	R	A	N	M	U	S	D	A	R	O
L	I	K	I	A	B	E	J	K	L	S	E	S	E	S
O	B	A	J	K	I	N	D	O	H	O	N	A	L	F
E	Y	H	T	R	O	W	T	S	U	R	T	C	A	L

p. 146 Crime-Fighting Crossword

p. 150 Green Arrow to the Rescue!